Evaluation Utilization

John A. McLaughlin, *Editor*
Virginia Tech

Larry J. Weber, *Editor*
Virginia Tech

Robert W. Covert, *Editor*
University of Virginia

Robert B. Ingle, *Editor*
University of Wisconsin

NEW DIRECTIONS FOR PROGRAM EVALUATION

A Publication of the American Evaluation Association

*A joint organization of the Evaluation Research Society
and the Evaluation Network*

MARK W. LIPSEY, *Editor-in-Chief*
Claremont Graduate School

Number 39, Fall 1988

Paperback sourcebooks in
The Jossey-Bass Higher Education and
Social and Behavioral Sciences Series

H
61
.E95x
west

Jossey-Bass Inc., Publishers
San Francisco • London

John A. McLaughlin, Larry J. Weber, Robert W. Covert,
Robert B. Ingle (eds.).
Evaluation Utilization.
New Directions for Program Evaluation, no. 39.
San Francisco: Jossey-Bass, 1988.

New Directions for Program Evaluation Series
A publication of the American Evaluation Association
Mark W. Lipsey, *Editor-in-Chief*

New Directions for Program Evaluation is published quarterly by
Jossey-Bass Inc., Publishers (publication number USPS 449-050),
and is sponsored by the American Evaluation Association.
Second-class postage rates are paid at San Francisco, California,
and at additional mailing offices. POSTMASTER: Send address
changes to Jossey-Bass Inc., Publishers, 350 Sansome Street,
San Francisco, California 94104.

Editorial correspondence should be sent to the Editor-in-Chief,
Mark Lipsey, Psychology Department, Claremont Graduate School,
Claremont, Calif. 91711.

Library of Congress Catalog Card Number LC 85-644749

International Standard Serial Number ISSN 0164-7989

International Standard Book Number ISBN 1-55542-894-0

Cover art by WILLI BAUM

Manufactured in the United States of America. Printed on acid-free paper.

Ordering Information

The paperback sourcebooks listed below are published quarterly and can be ordered either by subscription or single copy.

Subscriptions cost $60.00 per year for institutions, agencies, and libraries. Individuals can subscribe at the special rate of $45.00 per year *if payment is by personal check.* (Note that the full rate of $60.00 applies if payment is by institutional check, even if the subscription is designated for an individual.) Standing orders are accepted.

Single copies are available at $14.95 when payment accompanies order. (California, New Jersey, New York, and Washington, D.C., residents please include appropriate sales tax.) For billed orders, cost per copy is $14.95 plus postage and handling.

Substantial discounts are offered to organizations and individuals wishing to purchase bulk quantities of Jossey-Bass sourcebooks. Please inquire.

Please note that these prices are for the calendar year 1988 and are subject to change without prior notice. Also, some titles may be out of print and therefore not available for sale.

To ensure correct and prompt delivery, all orders must give either the *name of an individual* or an *official purchase order number.* Please submit your order as follows:

Subscriptions: specify series and year subscription is to begin.
Single Copies: specify sourcebook code (such as, PE1) and first two words of title.

Mail orders for United States and Possessions, Latin America, Canada, Japan, Australia, and New Zealand to:
Jossey-Bass Inc., Publishers
350 Sansome Street
San Francisco, California 94104

Mail orders for all other parts of the world to:
Jossey-Bass Limited
28 Banner Street
London EC1Y 8QE

New Directions for Program Evaluation Series
Mark W. Lipsey, *Editor-in-Chief*

New Directions for Program Evaluation

A Quarterly Publication of the American Evaluation Association
(A Joint Organization of the Evaluation Research Society
and the Evaluation Network)

American Evaluation Association, 9555 Persimmon Tree Road, Potomac, MD 20854

Contents

Editors' Notes

The Evaluation Network (ENET) and the Evaluation Research Society (ERS) merged in 1986 to form the American Evaluation Association (AEA). The theme for the new organization's first conference was "What Have We Learned?" Conference presenters and participants from varied fields assessed the state of the evaluation enterprise. The primary results of these efforts were captured in Cordray, Bloom, and Light (1987) and Bloom, Cordray, and Light (1988).

While several complex and challenging issues were identified at the 1986 conference, one topic seemed to surface more often as we participated in the discussions: utilization of evaluations. Questions seemed to center on what factors promote or serve as barriers to utilization. This focus is not new. Evaluators have always been interested in utilization. Concern for utilization went beyond the basic need of evaluators to know that their work was worthwhile. Resources were and continue to be limited. If evaluations were not being used, then why waste assets that could be dedicated to program functions?

We have learned a lot about utilization, as evidenced by what occurred at the 1986 conference. Utilization has many faces. At times uses are easy to identify—that is, indicators are explicit, allowing the evaluator and program staff to logically link evaluation recommendations to program decisions. Or to put it another way, changes in programs that can be attributed to evaluation information can be observed. Resources are increased or decreased. Interventions are modified or terminated. New programs replace old programs.

On the other hand, we have discovered that tracing utilization can be difficult. Effects of evaluations can be implicit, and in these instances, evaluators and program staff must infer relationships between evaluation recommendations and program decisions. Questions that often are difficult to answer must be addressed. Have our evaluations changed the way people think about a program? How do program staff combine evaluation findings with other information to make decisions? What are the intended or unexpected uses of evaluations? Does use differ across varied settings? Can evaluators, program staff, and managers not only define potential uses but also design strategies to enhance utilization?

In response to these and other unanswered questions, AEA president Robert Covert charged the 1987 program chairs to center their conference theme on the utilization of evaluations. Interest centered on determining the existence of innovative practices to promote utilization as well as identifying current research on utilization. In this way we sought to

1

increase our knowledge of utilization and, specifically, to provide evaluators and clients with the means through which evaluations could be designed to support utilization.

This volume of *New Directions* serves as a vehicle to report the observations and practices of evaluators from a number of perspectives regarding the utilization of evaluations. Topical interest groups from AEA were invited to submit papers on the subject of utilization as it relates to their particular emphasis. Manuscripts from authors engaged in research on evaluation also were sought. The work represents a review of factors that promote or inhibit utilization and a compendium of new directions in examining utilization.

In Chapter One, M. F. Smith examines current thinking regarding the utilization of evaluation studies. Smith defines use as it relates to both client and evaluator expectations. Reasons for the continuing concern for utilization are presented as well as a review of factors that promote or serve as barriers to utilization. The measurement of use in various settings is discussed in terms of the design and conduct of evaluation.

In complex organizations, evaluators and program managers are faced with the task of deciding which among many program initiatives should be evaluated. In Chapter Two, Daniel B. Muscatello presents a framework that has been used in the Port Authority of New York and New Jersey to enable internal evaluators to develop an evaluation agenda that is reasonable in a limited resource agency. Multiple factors are incorporated in the system, including potential human and material costs as well as administrative, political, and legal constraints.

In Chapter Three, which addresses the potential value of evaluation for the health care profession, Tara D. Knott discusses problems associated with such evaluation gaining acceptance. She posits that utilization of health care evaluations too frequently receives low-priority status from persons having responsibility and authority to fund, instigate, and use them. Her chapter addresses the problems evaluators encounter with three major groups—physicians, hospital administrators, and patients—that can benefit from health care evaluation. The focus of the chapter is on strategies evaluators might use to acquire greater acceptance of their products from these client groups.

In Chapter Four, Carol T. Mowbray presents the perspective of working in a health-related area. Her solution to the problem, unlike Knott's (which is directed at specific client groups), involves the use of more generalized approaches that can have applicability to areas other than the health field. She talks about strategies to be used during various stages of an evaluation that should help ensure greater utilization. In the early stages, promotional efforts are emphasized. During the time when the evaluation is being conducted, the ways to involve individuals in the operations work of planning, design, and implementation receive attention. Finally, she focuses on ways to gain acceptance of evaluation results through novel and insightful interpretation of study results.

In Chapter Five, Oliver W. Cummings and colleagues discuss how two internal and external evaluation perspectives act on the utilization of evaluations. Professional evaluators who serve in three distinct evaluation roles—external evaluators, company evaluation department representatives, and evaluator members of a project team—respond to questions posed by a panel of evaluation experts. Factors such as cost, credibility, relationship to client, and quality control are discussed from the three reference points. Apparent commonalities and uniquenesses are presented. No one position surfaces as the ideal, but rather, the program context seems to be the determinant.

William P. Johnston, Jr., in Chapter Six on utilization of General Accounting Office (GAO) evaluations, found that contrary to most utilization studies, recommendations from GAO management performance evaluations were frequently used. Johnston notes factors contributing to use, including GAO's mission of effecting change in federal programs and its reputation as an organization that not only conducts management performance evaluations but also sets the standards for evaluating federal programs. This last factor is considered important because the findings of studies can be applied across multiple agencies. Johnston emphasizes that when utilization is viewed as change in the organizations, the extent of demand from change perceived by the target agencies is a major determinant of use.

Finally, in Chapter Seven, Michael Quinn Patton focuses on the cost of evaluations, citing the Joint Committee standard that the cost of the evaluation enterprise should not exceed its value to program staff. Drawing on his recent experiences with the evaluation of U.S. AID programs, Patton presents a model for integrating evaluation activities into program functions. According to the framework presented, evaluation does not have to be independent of the program. When they are separate, costs for the evaluation may be viewed as unreasonably high and, indeed, the evaluation results are less useful. Traditional evaluation procedures are contrasted with those where evaluation is more program oriented. In the former, evaluation costs are viewed as add-on costs while in the latter, they are considered as direct program costs. Finally, Patton discusses the role of internal and external evaluators in relation to data reporting and use.

The purpose of this *New Directions* volume is to provide a forum for the continued examination of the issues and practices associated with the utilization of program evaluations. As can be seen by our summary of chapter topics, readers will be exposed to both a review of old concepts and to new and emergent ideas about utilization. While summarization always suffers from a loss of rich information, we believe that some key concepts have been presented by the authors. These are listed below:

1. Utilization is an elusive concept that is most meaningful to stakeholders and evaluators of the target program. Concern for utilization must be addressed from the very early stages of the evaluation. Those involved in the evaluation must establish their perceptions of both intended and unintended uses. Will the evaluation result in instrumental or observable changes in the program operation or decisions to revise, disseminate, or terminate the program? Is the primary purpose to change people's vision of the program, or to serve as a legitimizing agent for the program? What are the short- and long-term uses of the evaluation by varied audiences.

The message that is heard repeatedly is that utilization is maximized when evaluators and stakeholders focus on potential uses as part of the evaluation plan. For each evaluation question, the purposes must be clearly defined.

2. In addition to conceptualizing use at the beginning of the evaluation, it is vital to establish mechanisms for tracking use. It is important to include an evaluation question that addresses the success of the evaluation in terms of use. Tracking systems should be put in place immediately. Even during the planning phase, the evaluation begins to have programmatic impact, which continues throughout the evaluation. Retrospective studies are less desirable because of the difficulty of identifying uses and attributing them to the evaluation.

3. Distinguishing between formative and summative purposes of evaluations affects utilization. While this is "old hat" for most of us, it bodes well for both evaluators and stakeholders to reflect on the underlying purposes for conducting the evaluation. These purposes affect our designs, investigative methodologies, and recommendations. Too frequently, evaluations are formulated in a summative or accountability mode that may focus more on negative facets of the program. At times, program staff, participants, and others are operating under the assumption that the purpose of the evaluation is formative—directed at program improvement—only to find later that summative, go/no-go decisions are the main objective. Utilization would be enhanced if studies were framed in a manner less threatening to those who are involved in the evaluation. Anticipated uses should be made public.

4. Evaluations often are conducted in complex political, economic, social, and administrative environments. Decision makers must use input from a number of sources, including evaluation reports. As such, it may be difficult to determine the relationship between evaluation findings and recommendations and decisions.

5. When merged with program functions, evaluation will be perceived as less costly because it serves as both an accountability tool and,

at the same time, informs staff and participants about future program directions. Evaluations that are more closely integrated with program activities are more likely to be used.

6. Evaluators must be proactive in regard to the acceptance of their evaluation. An important evaluator function is to sell the evaluation by informing program staff of its potential for current and future program decisions. Greater acceptance can be anticipated when the evaluator has a thorough understanding of user expectations and the context in which each user group operates.

In any organization there are a number of programs that compete for limited evaluation resources. While it is not possible to evaluate all programs in a given time period, it is possible to establish in-house systems for identifying those programs that will receive priority in the allocation of evaluation resources. Factors to consider are personnel and specialized resource costs; internal support for the evaluation; maturity of the program; clarity of the program description; and political, legislative, or administrative driving and restraining forces.

7. Utilization can be influenced through the use of pressure groups that seek benefits from the evaluation. It is valuable to find someone, preferably internal to the organization, to champion the evaluation. When program staff advocate for the evaluation, its use potential is enhanced. Employing the political process as a means for change has been neglected by evaluators. Including representatives from special interest groups as members of advisory teams, confidants, and supporters can help ensure that the results of evaluation efforts are not ignored or overlooked.

It is hard to think of a situation in which there is no planned or intended use of an evaluation. In a limited resource market, it would be difficult to justify evaluation costs without explicit purposes for such expenditures. In the following chapters, the authors present factors impinging on the design of evaluations that will lead to use.

John A. McLaughlin
Larry J. Weber
Robert W. Covert
Robert B. Ingle
Editors

References

Bloom, H. S., Cordray, D. S., and Light, R. J. (eds.). *Lessons from Selected Program and Policy Areas.* New Directions for Program Evaluation, no. 37. San Francisco: Jossey-Bass, 1988.

6

Cordray, D. S., Bloom, H. S., and Light, R. J. (eds.). *Evaluation Practice in Review.* New Directions for Program Evaluation, no. 34. San Francisco: Jossey-Bass, 1987.

-

John A. McLaughlin is associate professor and director of Virginia Tech's Institute for the Study of Exceptionalities. His evaluation interests focus on educational programs and products, particularly those directed at special needs populations.

Larry J. Weber is professor of education at Virginia Tech. For twenty-five years he has been involved in teacher education, curriculum and program development, and evaluation activities. He has consulted with international, national, state, and local educational agencies on matters pertaining to testing, evaluation, and instruction.

Robert W. Covert is associate professor in the Evaluation Research Center of Curry School of Education at the University of Virginia. He is the immediate past president of AEA, and his evaluation interests center on ethical considerations in the design, conduct, and reporting of evaluation studies.

Robert B. Ingle is professor of educational psychology at the University of Wisconsin. As the annual meeting chair for AEA and ENET, he has been a central figure in the organization since its inception. He has long been recognized for his work in the preparation of evaluation.

*While much is known about the form and practice of
evaluation across the public and private sectors of our
community, there remains a need to clarify the forces for
and against utilization of the results of program evaluation.
This chapter examines the reasons why evaluation use is of
interest and defines some of the many dimensions of use
as well as factors that influence planning for and
measuring use.*

Evaluation Utilization Revisited

M. F. Smith

Evaluation utilization is being questioned? Why now and why at all? The answer sounds like a Gallo wine advertisement: Because it is time! Evaluation as a profession meets two criteria for a useful impact study: a program has been implemented and for a sufficient time for results to have occurred. A third criterion for useful impact studies is also present: someone wants to know. Someone wants to know now because resources are scarcer than when program evaluation got its running start with the 1960s Great Society programs. If evaluation can be shown to have little or no positive program impact, the expense can be eliminated. Another reason may be that evaluation was oversold, and its limitations just now are becoming apparent. For example, evaluations cannot make decisions. They can provide data, identify strengths or weaknesses, and provide varied comparative information, but they cannot decide. Particularly, they are not much help in deciding "should" issues, which dominate policy making (Smith, 1987b). Evaluations may also lead to information overload; they can expand as well as narrow decision options (Stevenson, 1981).

What is a little surprising is that evaluators themselves are primary among those who are raising questions about utilization. This is surprising because utilization seems so obvious—that is, plain, common, self-evident, and maybe even simple. One reason utilization seems obvious

J. A. McLaughlin, L. J. Weber, R. W. Covert, and R. B. Ingle (eds.). *Evaluation Utilization.*
New Directions for Program Evaluation, no. 39. San Francisco: Jossey-Bass, Fall 1988.

involves the practical matter of knowing how to proceed. Without knowing intended use, how does one know what questions to ask, who or what to ask them of, and how soon they must be asked? It seems a logical first step. As Merwin (1983) pointed out, "It is difficult to conceive of the initiation of an evaluation without intent that due to the evaluation something will change, be it funding, program activities, attitudes, or understanding" (p. 7).

A second reason utilization seems obvious is based on my personal experiences as an internal evaluator of a public school system, a university health center, a college of education, a college of agriculture, and Cooperative Extension. When one is an internal evaluator, all studies are formative, from an organizational viewpoint (Stevenson, 1981). This means they are intended to have use for organizational improvement— whether they are descriptive, formative, or summative in actual design. In contrast, external evaluators have sometimes designed and conducted evaluations to satisfy criteria in a request for proposals. Granted, many of these evaluations may have had characteristics of design that could be viewed as more rigorous methodologically, but it is doubtful that they scored as well on the criteria of usefulness. By virtue of being closer to the programmatic situation, the internal evaluator has greater opportunity to make evaluations useful; "they understand the need to look good as well as the need to be good, and can often help with interpreting appropriately the same findings to different audiences" (Wright, 1987).

A third reason is that the profession has been discussing this topic for a number of years. As Steele (1987) wrote, "I am just a little weary with this topic." In 1980 when I reviewed the literature on utilization for a now-annual national institute on program evaluation (Smith, 1980), a host of evaluation utilization studies had already been conducted. For example, Patton and his associates (1975) had published their study of twenty health evaluations; Weiss, alone and with others, had come out with a number of publications on the topic (see Weiss, 1971, 1973; Weiss and Bucuvalas, 1977); Alkin and Daillak (1979) had categorized the critical factors of evaluation that affect utilization; and Patton (1978) had published a book on the subject *Utilization-Focused Evaluation*. This *New Directions* volume evidences the continued emphasis since 1980.

There is also a related body of literature that, through time, has paralleled the development of program evaluation. That literature is specifically about information use and technology transfer. For example, in 1962 Rogers published the famous research on adoption theory where he, and later he and Shoemaker (1971), described a process for individual adoption (awareness—>interest—>trial—>evaluation—>adoption) and a basis for prediction for group adoption (the so-called bell curve for innovators, early adopters, early majority, late majority, and laggards). The parallels to a discussion on evaluation utilization seem apparent.

The final reason for thinking utilization is obvious could be subconscious feelings of insecurity about the worth of my work, compensated for by exhibiting assessments of grandeur (that is, assessments of "obviousness"). Perhaps I (and the evaluation profession) am suffering a role identity crisis. Actually, Ernie House is responsible for this thought. In one of his delightful intellectual exercises that occur in each issue of *Evaluation Practice*, he described a group of young men on campus, dressed in gowns, passing out literature, chanting, playing musical instruments, heads shaven, and completely undaunted that day after day he passed right by them and refused to accept any of their literature or to listen to any of their messages (House, 1987). Each day they would be back doing the same things with the same vigor and fervor. House noted that they have a strong sense of their place in the world and of their need to change the world, and he wondered if we understood our role as clearly.

This utilization question to some extent could be likened to a debate on the evaluator's role in social change or a debate on utilization versus utility. In other words, is the role perceived as getting results used or is it to present them in such a way that they can be used? The former carries a responsibility for deciding what in programs is appropriate to be preserved for society and to be an advocate for those changes; the latter puts that responsibility in the hands of other decision makers. Does the profession have a strong sense of its identity? Do we know what "utilization" means?

The Many Faces of Utilization

There are many dimensions to the concept of utilization, especially if it is to be planned and measured. Such an opportunity was presented in the Cooperative Extension Service (CES) recently with the publication of the Futures Task Force report (1987). In that report, the task force made the following observation:

> Considerable attention has been directed toward the design and implementation of evaluation studies. However, no mechanism exists to facilitate the use of evaluation results in making decisions, reaching conclusions, or forming judgments about the effectiveness of Extension programming [p. 14].

They went on to recommend that a network be developed "by which results of impact studies and reports can be communicated to decision makers responsible for documenting the value of Extension programming" (p. 14).

The task force is calling for a system for planned utilization of evaluations in CES. Should CES decide to pursue that objective, four questions will need to be examined: (1) What are the boundaries? (2) What is meant by *use*? (3) What actions facilitate use? and (4) How can use be measured? These questions are discussed here in the context of the challenge presented by the CES Futures Task Force, but they are pertinent to any organizational context where evaluation utilization is promoted.

What Are the Boundaries? Decisions about levels and types of evaluations and of users are important not only for designing mechanisms for making utilization happen but also for determining that it does. Because evaluations and users are different, the general criteria for use should probably be different for evaluations focused at the national level than for local studies, as they probably should be for evaluations of infant as compared to fully mature programs and for formative as compared to summative evaluations (Stevenson, 1981; Patton, 1985). The same would be true for users. The needs of the user located in the federal office are usually much different from those of the user located in a county office. Similarly, the needs of the user working with legislative committees differ from the user working with commodity committees. In spite of these differences, though, some utilization criteria can be generalized—that is, not all criteria are specific to the individual evaluation nor to the individual user.

What Is Meant by "Use"? The literature on utilization is replete with definitions of use as a multidimensional concept. Chelimsky (1983) compounded this complexity when she said, "The concept of usefulness . . . depends upon the perspective and values of the observer. This means that one person's usefulness may be another person's waste." (p. 155). Patton (1985) echoed the same sentiments when he said, "There can be no absolute standard which values action over thinking, changes in a program over keeping things the same, or decisions to do something over decisions to wait. There simply can be no hierarchy of impacts, because the hierarchy is necessarily situational and depends on the values and the needs of the people for whom the evaluation is conducted" (p. 7). Four ways that use has been conceptualized by different writers include directly observable versus perceptual, process versus product, partial versus holistic, and immediate versus long term.

Directly Observable Versus Perceptual. A number of writers discuss evaluation use from these two perspectives, though the terminology may be slightly different. For instance, Cooley and Bickel (1986) have referred to instrumental and conceptual use (documentable to specific decisions and influencing policy makers' thinking, respectively), Patton (1985, 1986) has discussed action and conceptual impacts (leading to observable changes in actual operations of a program and affecting thinking about a program, respectively). Chelimsky (1987) prioritized the two when she indicated that the main value of evaluation to policy "is not its capacity for political influence but its contribution of systematic, independent, critical thinking to the decision making process" (p. 11). Steele (1987) suggested a frequency of occurrence: "Some uses can be directly traced . . . but more often evaluations are blended into a person's total knowledge base and add to what one generally knows and believes about a topic" (p. 1). Patton (1985) seemed to be suggesting some kind of middle ground when he said, "A decision to do absolutely nothing new or different can be a major evaluation impact but will not lead to any observable action or change as a result of the evaluation" (p. 7); however, one might argue that the decision to do nothing was a result of someone's critical thinking having been affected.

Process Versus Results. Process impact means that something happens to a program and to people involved in an evaluation, which is over and above any predicted impact from the program (Merwin, 1983). Going through the process of designing an evaluation stimulates staff to think rigorously about their program in ways that might have happened without the forced stimulus of coming to grips with the demands of the evaluation (Patton, 1985). That has certainly been true in evaluability assessments conducted in Cooperative Extension. Smith (1987a) reported examples in Illinois and California where, as evaluations were proceeding, programs have changed to the extent that some of the evaluability assessment questions (design plausibility) became irrelevant.

Immediate Versus Long Term. Evaluation use may be compared to use of books in a library (Oliver, 1987). Some books may collect dust on shelves until the moment someone needs that specific information. Similarly with evaluation studies. We do them, write them up, and establish a reservoir of information. We do not always know which studies will be useful or when, but as the need arises, we "check them out." This happens over and over by different library (evaluator) patrons. This reservoir of evaluation results provides a capability and data base for increasing institutional knowledge and memory.

Partial/Incremental Versus Holistic. Oliver (1987) accused evaluators of assuming their studies should be holistically accepted: "They make an assumption that one action (their study) will cause another, and that isn't always the case." Weiss's (1980) description of organizational decision making suggests this concept of use is important for success: "A lot of different people in a lot of different offices go about their work taking small steps without consideration of the total issue or the long-term consequences. Through a series of seemingly small and uncoordinated actions, things happen . . . over a period of time [and] these many steps crystallize into a change in direction" (p. 76–77). Patton (1986) spoke similarly when he said, "there are few major, direction-changing decisions in most programming. . . . Evaluation research is used as one piece of information that feeds into a slow evolutionary process of program development. Program development is a process of 'muddling through' . . . and program evaluation is part of that muddling" (p. 36).

These four dimensions of use are sufficient for a conclusion that facilitation of use is dependent on and complicated by how *use* is defined. An action that will facilitate one use may not facilitate another.

What Actions Facilitate Use? Evaluators and organizations implement actions that encourage or hinder utilization—that is, what the evaluator does and how the context in which it is done affect use. Examples of both are discussed here, beginning with the evaluator.

Evaluator Actions. Two considerations in evaluation design—which may be labeled as actions—are most important for maximum use to occur: using program theory as a basis for design and taking a client or stakeholder orientation. Using program theory means that causal links between the operation of the program and its intended effects are identified (Bickman, 1987). This should be the responsibility of program developers but many times is not in evidence prior to an evaluation. Identifying causal links in a program can (1) contribute to our understanding about how people and organizations interact for problem amelioration; (2) determine if failure to show positive impact is a failure of how the program is implemented or, rather, a result of applying the wrong program for a particular audience or problem; (3) uncover unintended effects; (4) identify portions of a program that contribute to success; and (5) enable the selection of variables and measures most valid for the program and the questions being asked (Bickman, 1987).

A number of writers have indicated the profound importance of the second most important action for maximum utilization of evaluations: taking a client or stakeholder orientation (see Baker, 1983; Cooley, 1983; Eash, 1985; Siegel and Tuckel, 1985; Cooley and Bickel, 1986; Patton, 1986; Chelimsky, 1987). A client orientation requires the following: identifying the specific primary clients or stakeholders and involving them in all phases of the design from identification of specific information needs to strategies for obtaining that information to analyzing and disseminating results. The more involved the stakeholder becomes with the evaluation, the more targeted its results will be, and thus the more used those results will be. Important in this orientation, though, is the identification of the primary stakeholders. Evaluations that try to serve everyone's needs for information may end up serving no one very effectively.

Over and above this involvement of the client/stakeholder in all phases of the evaluation is the assumption that the evaluator will take an educative approach to the client relative to the evaluation process (Eash, 1985; Patton, 1985). Such an approach involves more than outlining alternatives for clients and getting their participation in decision making. Rather, it involves educating decision makers in evaluation processes and the uses of information. Actually, this endeavor can be mutually beneficial. The evaluator can become as knowledgeable as possible about the program while helping the decision makers to become as sophisticated as is feasible about evaluation.

Evaluator strategies for stimulating use are presented in Exhibit 1. Some of these are included or implied in the program theory and stakeholder orientations already mentioned, but those considerations are much broader than these individual strategies and less action specific. Exhibit 1 can be summarized as follows: make sure that data are collected and reported so as to clearly answer questions—do not leave the decision makers guessing; provide data about variables that can be manipulated; present findings as prescriptions for future use; and, finally, couch information within the context of other relevant work.

Exhibit 1. Evaluator Facilitating Actions

1. Consider utilization at every evaluation decision point. By the end of the evaluation, the potential for use has been largely determined (Merwin, 1983; Patton, 1986).

2. Answer the questions that are asked (Patton, 1986); credibility involves more than methodological quality, it involves responsiveness to the specific policy question and information need (Chelimsky, 1987). Focus data gathering on those factors amenable both to manipulation and to intervention with program efforts (Baker, 1983; Weiss and Bucuvalas, 1977; Chelimsky, 1987).

3. Frame findings in terms of the intended users; findings in unfamiliar categories and concepts make it difficult for the potential users to translate them into action alternatives (Baker, 1983; Siegel and Tuckel, 1985; Patton, 1985). Closely related to this is Weiss and Bucuvalas's (1977) discovery of a major construct of use called "conformity of user expectations": the likelihood of users valuing a report increases when the findings agree with the users' construction of reality.

4. Focus recommendations on incremental rather than global changes; smaller-scale changes are likely to be less disruptive and less likely to meet with resistance (Rothman, 1980; Siegel and Tuckel, 1985).

5. State recommendations as goals (ends) rather than delineating specific courses of action; people may be more willing to do something if they retain control over how it is done (Siegel and Tuckel, 1985).

6. State recommendations in prescriptive terms. Evaluators look back, and decision makers look forward; decision makers want to know what the findings signify for future programming actions (Chelimsky, 1987).

7. Make sure there is an obvious nexus between the recommendations and the data; otherwise the recommendations may be conceived as ideologically or politically inspired (and mistrusted) (Siegel and Tuckel, 1985).

8. Avoid, as much as possible, calling into question the organization's beliefs and value system (Siegel and Tuckel, 1985).

9. Adhere to rigorous methodological standards of practice (Weiss and Bucuvalas, 1977). A common strategy of those who oppose report findings is to discredit the methods (Siegel and Tuckel, 1985). Credibility is the "sine qua non of use over the long term" (Chelimsky, 1987, p. 14).

Exhibit 1. *(continued)*

10. Use a combination of approaches and methods to secure information so that the strengths of one can mitigate the weaknesses of another (Chelimsky, 1987).

11. Time presentations of findings to the decisions to be affected (Siegel and Tuckel, 1985).

12. Make findings clear, useful, and effectively available to policymakers. This means ordering them in a policy context, condensing, trimming surgically what is not relevant. Telling all in the same neutral tone can be tantamount to telling nothing. Do not leave it to the policymaker to perceive the areas of success (Weiss and Bucuvalas, 1977; Rothman, 1980; Chelimsky, 1978). Light and Pillemer (1984) made a similar recommendation about providing policymakers with only what is pertinent: "Our policy makers do not lack advice; they are in many respects overwhelmed by it" (p. 17).

13. Rediscover the anecdote. After getting a sense of the size of a problem, of its range, its frequency, its direction, and its average characteristics, one of the most effective ways to present findings in the political forum is to illustrate the general findings via specific cases and analogies that graphically focus attention on, or explain, the large points (Chelimsky, 1987). Anecdotes should not be presented as the only data but are effective when used in conjunction with the more generalizable data.

14. Reduce political barriers (Smith, 1987b). Become thoroughly familiar with the political process, operate within it, recognize the political viability of possible solutions, and know what means are politically acceptable for getting the solutions implemented. Be flexible and adaptable in interactions with politically significant players—compromise is the key to achievement; demonstrate a willingness to consider others' views on matters of mutual interest.

15. Couch findings within the context of other work done in the area (Ciarlo, 1981; Stevenson, 1981; U.S. General Accounting Office, 1983). Reviewing literature is important before a study is designed but is often omitted in the interest of time or because of the mistaken belief that evaluative information is decision maker specific. "The ability to draw on a large number of soundly designed and executed studies adds great strength to the knowledge base when findings are consistent across different studies conducted by different analysts using different methods. No single study, no matter how good, can have this kind of power" (U.S. General Accounting Office, 1983, p. 1).

Any student of learning theory and adoption theory will see very little new information in the identified use-facilitating actions concerning how to encourage adult learning and adoption of technology. For example, Wolek (1985) reviewed a large body of published, empirical, and theoretical studies about technology transfer and distilled three principles of effective transfer: (1) mutual definition of the technology by those who will perform the research and development and the producer/ users; (2) interdependent action in the interpretation, direction setting, and risk taking involved in developing the technology; and (3) network dissemination of information by opinion leaders, experts, and change agents. Wolek concluded that "if technology transfer is to be effective, it must be aimed at a specific group of users/producers who have a clear need which they have defined and who will be involved throughout the R&D and dissemination processes. . . . In other words, just as technology must be designed in interaction with its targeted users, so should a dissemination program be designed and promoted by its appropriate network" (pp. 58, 66).

Organizational Influencers. The administrative/management framework or infrastructure for evaluation within an organization can significantly influence evaluation success. Cooley and Bickel (1986) suggest the thorough integration of an organization's research (evaluation) capacity with its decision and policy processes. This means that the evaluation resource has reasonable access to key management and policy-shaping actors in the system. The purpose of the access is for two-way communication: for the evaluation resource to be cognizant of information needs and for decision makers to acquire research-generated knowledge. Such an infrastructure would provide the best situation for use of information to occur: the information is shared informally and verbally as discussions occur where the generated information is relevant. Of course, this does not preclude the more formal presentations but has the advantage of "striking when the iron is hot."

Different organizational arrangements may provide "reasonable access." Carlson (1979) suggests that evaluative units are more productive and useful when they report directly to the top person in the organization. "The more bureaucratic layers there are between the full-time manager of the evaluation group and the principal policy maker the group serves, the greater the prospects that study results will not be responsive, timely, and used in critical decisions, and the more difficult it will be to sustain high-grade professional analytical work over time" (p. 77).

Other facilitating organizational actions include:

1. Setting overall boundaries of the evaluation capacity and defining "legitimate tasks" within the context of organization excellence (Carlson, 1979).

2. Consolidating scarce evaluation resources and targeting to priority areas (Smith, 1987b). Priorities should be considered carefully in the shaping and use of any valued, finite resource and should be managed in ways to produce the greatest benefit. This requires a central coordinating capability with access to key administrative decisions and to key management resources.

3. Targeting results to all management levels (Smith, 1987b). The most useful data assist management at all levels—not just the top level. One reason is that the actual decisions affected by evaluative information are more likely to be made at middle and lower management levels. Another reason is that to survive and be able to continue to collect relevant information requires that individuals from all levels see it as helpful. This also requires a central coordinating capability.

All these different actions suggest that it may be time to change the often recommended formula for planning allotment of time for evaluations. The old formula is that one-third of the total time available for evaluation be budgeted for design, one-third for implementation, and one-third for preparing the report. Perhaps a portion should likewise be set aside for encouraging utilization of evaluation findings and processes. Some guidance as to what that portion should be may be gleaned from the Stevenson-Wydler Act (the National Innovation Act of 1980), which called for all R&D agencies to set aside 5 percent of their funds to promote the transfer of results to industry (Wolek, 1985).

How Can Use Be Measured? Attempts to estimate extent of impact should take into account all dimensions of impact that can be identified (Merwin, 1983). Similar sentiment is offered by almost all the other authors cited in this chapter—as is evident from the earlier discussion on what constitutes use. But to design a way of assessing use, assumptions have to be made about similarities either in specific potential use or in classes or types of use.

One approach could be to require each evaluation to have included in its design the criteria and standards by which to judge the extent of its use and to have included in its implementation plan the ways to determine if that use ensued. "Accomplishment would then be judged on the basis of how well actual utilization indicators were demonstrated" (Tedrick, 1987, p. 1). This would accommodate the situation specificity of individual evaluations. It would not, however, easily accommodate timely reporting of evaluations and demonstration of incremental and long-term use. National or state-level aggregations would incur the same problems as presently experienced with aggregation of program impact—that is, few evaluations reporting on the same variables. However, the data could be used for accountability purposes—to say that resources are not being wasted on unused evaluations. Samples of evaluations could be selected and judgments of accountability made on the individual cases and summed to arrive at some overall success rate, for example, x percent of the evaluations met x level in planned use.

Other approaches also could be used. In fact, there are probably as many ways to measure evaluation utilization as there are ways to measure program impact, once what is to be measured is fully defined. For example, stakeholders could by surveyed to determine if and in what ways they "used" evaluations and their satisfaction or dissatisfaction with the use; or a set of criteria could be defined and a survey made of evaluation designs and reports to determine probable or actual use, and so on.

Conclusion

Different dimensions of evaluation utilization have been discussed within the context of designing a formal system for that purpose. However, pursuance of such a goal could have negative results. For example, any systematic approach to accounting for evaluation impact would probably cut down on a number of unused evaluations—in the traditional definition of *use*. On the other hand, it could also decrease our potential to continue to create and update our knowledge about programming and how to solve social problems. The fear is that an "official" system would place great value on directly observable action and ignore the conceptual and perceptual uses that contribute substantially to our thinking.

I believe utilization is a function of design, and that the need exists to improve the design process. For some evaluations this means more quality involvement of the primary stakeholders throughout the entire evaluation. For others, it means closer adherence to rigorous methodological standards of practice so that credibility is assured. Both of these do not have to exist to the same extent in each evaluation, since data for specific decisions may not have to meet the same rigorous standards as that for creation of new knowledge.

This separation is somewhat contrary to the literature on utilization. In nearly every article, either explicitly or implicitly, there is the expectation that evaluations should meet decision makers' needs. However, I agree with Morrill and Francis (1979), who said the chief administrator does not have to be consulted on every evaluation, nor do all possible future decisions have to be identified prior to selecting studies, nor does every study have to be targeted to specific decisions. Craig Oliver (1987) director of extention at the University of Maryland, suggested that evaluators perceive their function, at least in part, as one of creating a repository of knowledge. Morrill and Francis (1979) described that function most eloquently when they said,

> Creation of knowledge is a gradual process, and the results of many studies as well as of simple facts, values, and the like will usually be pertinent to any single issue or decision. . . . While each evaluation should be carefully tailored in the light of past studies and anticipated future uses (plural), there is no simple or mechanical formula for achieving this end" [p. 37].

References

Alkin, M. C., and Daillak, R. H. "A Study of Evaluation Utilization." *Educational Evaluation and Policy Analysis*, 1979, *1* (4), 41–49.

Baker, E. L. "Tests and the Real World." In S. J. Hueftle (ed.), *The Utilization of Evaluation. Proceedings of the Minnesota Evaluation Conference*. Minneapolis: Minnesota Research and Evaluation Center, 1983.

Bickman, L. "The Functions of Program Theory." In L. Bickman (ed.), *Using Program Theory in Evaluation*. New Directions for Program Evaluation, no. 33. San Francisco: Jossey-Bass, 1987.

Carlson, W. A. "The Management of Outcome Evaluation." In G. R. Gilbert and P. J. Conklin (eds.), *Evaluation Management: A Selection of Readings*. Washington, D.C.: Federal Executive Institute, U.S. Office of Personnel Management, 1979.

Chelimsky, E. "Improving the Cost Effectiveness of Evaluation." In M. C. Alkin and L. C. Solmon (eds.), *The Costs of Evaluation*. Newbury Park, Calif.: Sage, 1983.

Chelimsky, E. "What Have We Learned About the Politics of Program Evaluation?" *Evaluation Practice*, 1987, *8* (1), 5–21.

Ciarlo, J. A. (ed.). *Utilizing Evaluation*. Newbury Park, Calif.: Sage, 1981.

Cooley, W. W. "The Difference Between the Evaluation Being Used and the Evaluator Being Used." In S. J. Hueftle (ed.), *The Utilization of Evaluation. Proceedings of the Minnesota Evaluation Conference*. Minneapolis: Minnesota Research and Evaluation Center, 1983.

Cooley, W., and Bickel, W. *Decision-Oriented Educational Research*. Boston: Kluwer-Nijhoff, 1986.

Eash, M. J. "Evaluation Research and Program Evaluation Retrospect and Prospect: A Reformulation of the Role of the Evaluator." Paper presented at the Annual Meeting of the American Educational Research Association, Chicago, Mar. 31–Apr. 4, 1985.

Futures Task Force. *Extension in Transition: Bridging the Gap Between Vision and Reality*. Washington, D.C.: Extension Committee on Organization and Policy, Extension Service, U.S. Department of Agriculture, 1987.

House, E. "Evaluators, Libs, and Neocons." *Evaluation Practice*, 1987, *8* (1), 64–67.

Light, R. J., and Pillemer, D. B. *"Summing Up": The Science of Reviewing Research*. Cambridge, Mass.: Harvard University Press, 1984.

Merwin, J. C. "Dimensions of Evaluation Impact." In S. J. Hueftle (ed.), *The Utilization of Evaluation. Proceedings of the Minnesota Evaluation Center*. Minneapolis: Minnesota Research and Evaluation Center, 1983.

Morrill, W. A., and Francis, W. J. "Evaluation from the HEW Perspective." In G. R. Gilbert and P. J. Conklin (eds.), *Evaluation Management: A Selection of Readings*. Washington, D.C.: Federal Executive Institute, U.S. Office of Personnel Management, 1979.

Oliver, C., director, Cooperative Extension Service, University of Maryland, College Park. Personal communication, Sept. 24, 1987.

Patton, M. Q. *Utilization-Focused Evaluation*. Newbury Park, Calif.: Sage, 1978.

Patton, M. Q. "Six Honest Serving Men for Evaluation." Paper presented at the Annual Meeting of the American Educational Research Association, Chicago, Mar. 31–Apr. 4, 1985.

Patton, M. Q. *Utilization-Focused Evaluation*. (2nd ed.) Newbury Park, Calif.: Sage, 1986.

Patton, M. Q., Grimes, P. S., Guthrie, K. M., Brennan, N. J., French, B. D., and Blyth, D. A. "In Search of Impact: An Analysis of the Utilization of Federal Health Evaluation Research." Minneapolis: Minnesota Center for Social Research, University of Minnesota, 1975.

Rogers, E. M. *Diffusion of Innovation*. New York: Free Press, 1962.

Rogers, E. M., and Shoemaker, F. F. *Communication of Innovations, A Cross-Cultural Approach*. New York: Free Press, 1971.

Rothman, J. *Using Research in Organizations: A Guide to Successful Application*. Newbury Park, Calif.: Sage, 1980.

Siegel, K., and Tuckel, P. "The Utilization of Evaluation Research, A Case Analysis." *Evaluation Review*, 1985, *9* (3), 307–328.

Smith, M. F. "Evaluation Utilization Influences." Paper presented at the First Annual Winter Institute on Evaluating Cooperative Extension Programs, Orlando, Fla., Mar. 7-11, 1980.

Smith, M. F. *Evaluability Assessment, Reconciling Rhetoric with Reality.* Unpublished manuscript. College of Agriculture, University of Maryland, College Park, 1987a.

Smith, M. F. "Managing Evaluations for Effectiveness." Paper presented at the ECOP-Sponsored National Extension Conference for Evaluation, San Antonio, Tex., Mar. 25-27, 1987b.

Steele, S., professor and program development specialist, University of Wisconsin-Extension. Personal communication, Aug. 31, 1987.

Stevenson, J. F. "Assessing Evaluation Utilization in Human Service Agencies." In J. A. Ciarlo (ed.), *Utilizing Evaluation.* Newbury Park, Calif.: Sage, 1981.

Tedrick, B., evaluation specialist, Texas Cooperative Extension Service, University of Texas, College Station. Personal communication, Aug. 28, 1987.

U.S. General Accounting Office. *The Evaluation Synthesis.* Washington, D.C.: Institute for Program Evaluation, U.S. General Accounting Office, 1983.

Weiss, C. H. "Utilization of Evaluation: Toward Comparative Study." In F. G. Caro (ed.), *Readings in Evaluation Research.* New York: Russell Sage Foundation, 1971.

Weiss, C. H. "Where Politics and Evaluation Research Meet." *Evaluation,* 1973, *1* (3), 37-45.

Weiss, C. H. "An EEPA Interview with Carol H. Weiss." *Educational Evaluation and Policy Analysis,* 1980, *2* (5), 75-79.

Weiss, C. H., and Bucuvalas, M. J. *Social Science Research and Decision Making.* New York: Columbia University Press, 1977.

Wolek, F. W. "Transferring Federal Technology in Agriculture." *Journal of Technology Transfer,* 1985, *9* (2), 57-70.

Wright, J., associate professor, University of California, Davis. Personal communication, August 1987, October 1987.

M. F. Smith is associate professor and coordinator of program evaluation for the University of Maryland Cooperative Extension Service. She has been instrumental in the study of the utilization of evaluation research addressing Cooperative Extension Service programs.

In complex organizations there often are a number of programs that could benefit from evaluation. But which should be selected for study when evaluation resources are limited? This chapter presents one framework that could be utilized to identify programs with the highest potential for payoff to management resulting from evaluation. Criteria for assessing evaluation need are presented as well as standards for prioritizing programs to be evaluated.

Developing an Agenda That Works: The Right Choice at the Right Time

Daniel B. Muscatello

Often program evaluators are perceived and received with skepticism and suspicion. Knowing this, we all need to be extremely aware of the environment in which we operate, its potential for change, and its impact on the work we undertake.

Evaluators come from different areas—academia, the public sector, and the private sector. Some of us are research oriented, some of us are heavily involved in theoretical work, and others, such as my group at the Port Authority of New York and New Jersey, work with a bottom-line orientation. We all serve different masters with different interests and different areas of focus, but we all have a common goal: clear, conclusive, objective evaluations. However, that goal may not always be enough.

In complex organizations it is sometimes difficult to identify the projects or programs to evaluate. We must sort through the competing interests and priorities: In a limited resource market not all programs can be evaluated at once. An evaluation agenda must be developed. This chapter describes one process that may lead to the right choice at the right time.

J. A. McLaughlin, L. J. Weber, R. W. Covert, and R. B. Ingle (eds.). *Evaluation Utilization.*
New Directions for Program Evaluation, no. 39. San Francisco: Jossey-Bass, Fall 1988.

Context

The Port Authority of New York and New Jersey is a bi-state agency that reports to the governors of both states. Through a board of twelve commissioners (six from each state), it operates with a high level of autonomy and functions as a quasi-corporate entity focusing on transportation and economic development in the New York/New Jersey metropolitan area.

The organization's structure is divided into four primary business areas, each with its own unique but complementary mission: aviation, trans-Hudson, port, and world trade/economic development. These are supported by a variety of staff functions that in combination form an organization of 9,000 employees in eighteen separate departments with an operating budget of more than $2 billion and a five-year capital plan that projects expenditures of nearly $6 billion. Since the agency is self-supporting, to help maintain our business segments in optimum working condition and to be able to generate the financing for the massive capital plan, a program evaluation group was created to evaluate segments of the organization's business. Its mission is to

- Measure whether or not existing programs are meeting goals and objectives and propose alternatives as appropriate
- Evaluate the continuing need for a program in light of changing organization goals
- Evaluate the need for modification of an existing policy or practice.

A program is defined as an activity or group of activities that the organization has undertaken in order to implement its strategies and achieve its goals. It should, however, be identifiable as a discrete function, the efficiency and effectiveness of which can be measured in terms of its overall contribution to the organization's business plan.

In order to maximize utilization, a program evaluation function needs several things. First, the executive offices of the organization must be committed to evaluation, see it as part of the management team, and support it vigorously. This provides the credibility on which the implementation of recommendations resulting from the evaluation can be built. Second, the organization itself has to buy into the process in order to obtain the level of cooperation that individual program analysts need. Lastly, the program evaluation function must be seperate from other elements of the business planning process in order to maintain a neutral posture. If it is too closely connected to the budget process, evaluation will be perceived as a mere extension of that process, the main occupation of which is second guessing its recommendation.

Evaluation Topics

The program evaluation group usually does not lack potential topics from which to form an agenda. Suggestions can and do come from a number of sources. The executive offices of the organization provide input on a continuing basis as their own priorities and concerns change, and the director of the budget process suggests topics based on feedback from staff involved in the budget and business planning components of the organization.

Further, individual departments may identify areas, either specific to themselves or of a cross-cutting nature, that are suitable for program evaluators. Lastly, the program review group surfaces potential topics through two channels: (1) reviews of business plans to identify areas that might indicate the need for a more intense focus on that aspect of the agency's or department's business and (2) an established cyclical review of all organization programs.

Developing an Agenda

After coming up with a list of potential evaluation topics, the challenge is to develop a realistic agenda on which projected work load and staffing requirements can be based. This is much easier said than done. There are always a number of items of major import competing with each other for the relatively scarce staff resources available for designing and performing evaluations.

In our business we have to deal with the bottom line, and that means a couple of things. First, we have to take a good hard look at the value of the programs we evaluate, and second, we have to make sure that our own function carries its weight in the organization by conducting reviews and evaluations that are meaningful, implementable, and timely. Therefore, the evaluator must carefully outline the purpose and scope of the evaluation as well as those concerns that may exceed the immediate scope of the review. By developing an understanding of the relationship of the environmental and human issues to the scope, the analyst can better understand how difficult and important the study will be.

Input should, whenever possible, be obtained from the managers of programs under consideration for review. Not only will this approach help later to establish the priority of reviews, but also it will assist in marketing the value of program evaluation by obtaining buy-in. The evaluation process should convey a positive image so that the units affected by the studies perceive resulting changes to a program as beneficial.

It is important that criteria related to short- or long-term agency goals are utilized to determine which evaluations will be undertaken and the priority order in which they will be accomplished. Priorities are tied to broad issues such as the budget, capital projects, operational concerns, patron safety, community relations and cost-effectiveness. Specific criteria have been developed to assist executive management in determining these priorities. Weighted in the decision-making process are such considerations as how the results of a review will be used, the possibility of conducting the review from both an operational and staffing perspective, the viability of the implementation recommendations, and time constraints.

It is critical to be able to systematically assess potential work load and make planning decisions early in the process. Once a broad list of topics (there may be as many as fifty) has been developed, each evaluator is given two weeks to do some quick research on a subset of topics. At the end of that time, all evaluators meet to discuss and examine potential review areas. Typically, half of the proposed topics fall out as being nonissues or issues that can be addressed through other means. Topic assessment criteria are applied to the ones that remain to create a grid (Figure 1), which allows the difficulty of each evaluation to be individually and quantitatively examined. This will usually reduce the total of possible evaluation topics by half, forming an excellent basis for planning evaluation work and estimating resource requirements.

Remember, though, these criteria are planning tools, and there is nothing mysterious about them. They simply represent a way for an evaluation unit to systematically examine and compare the variables involved with proposed topics for future review. The weights work for this organization at this time. For another organization, a totally different emphasis might be appropriate. The criteria for the selection of topics are shown in Exhibit 1.

Prioritizing Program Evaluation Topics

Assessing the difficulty of proposed topics helps determine what can be done with the resources available to the unit. By applying a second set of criteria, evaluators can make judgments about the scheduling of the agenda and link program evaluation to executive management priorities in a way that will maximize the utility of both the individual evaluations and the unit itself. Completing Figure 2 assists in this process. These prioritization criteria enable us to express numerically the things that many evaluators routinely consider. The last category, "Difficulty of Evaluation," incorporates the summary assessment rating into the overall equation of management planning and prioritization. Once again, lowest totals indicate highest priorities. The rating scales for the six criteria are listed in Exhibit 2.

Conclusion

This chapter described a framework enabling internal evaluations to set an evaluation agenda. It was based on the premise that in large and perhaps even small organizations, there are a number of program initiatives that might be evaluated. A word of caution regarding the use of the framework: as in any data-gathering initiative, the resultant information must be interpreted in order to acquire meaning. The data that are recorded on the forms set forth in Figures 1 and 2 are reviewed and interpreted by both the evaluators and organization executives. It is from this review that meaning and utility are given to the rating effort.

Successful development of an evaluation agenda depends on two critical concepts. The first is the ability to see things in the real world as shades of gray as opposed to the black and white of theory. Alternatives must be considered with a clear and open mind, and the evaluator must

Figure 1. Potential Evaluation Topics Criteria
Topic

CRITERIA	A	B	C	D	E	F
Completion Time (1-5 Points)						
Cost of Materials (1-5 Points)						
Staffing Costs (1-5 Points)						
Resistance (2-10 Points)						
Program Purpose (1-5 Points)						
Program Maturity (1-5 Points)						
Program Definition (1-5 Points)						
Measurement Validity (1-5 Points)						
Measurement Reliability (1-5 Points)						
Administrative Constraints (2-10 Points)						
Political Constraints (2-10 Points)						
Legal Constraints (2-10 Points)						
Total Rating Points (16-80)						

Notes: Carefully consider any rating of 5 or 10; lower point totals equate to easier evaluation.

Exhibit 1. Program Evaluation Topic Assessment Criteria

Twelve criteria are utilized to assess the degree of difficulty associated with the evaluation of a program. Eight criteria have a range of 1 to 5, and four are doubled in impact, having a range of 2 to 10. A low rating is preferable since it indicates lower costs, less time, and fewer problems over the course of the evaluation. Totals may range from 16 to 80. Typically, the following summary rating distributions will apply with regard to determining whether or not to initiate a program evaluation.

Summary Assessment

Rating	Comments
16–30	No anticipated problems with the evaluation.
31–45	Some minor problems or slightly escalated staffing or material costs should be anticipated.
46–60	The evaluation will be somewhat difficult and/or costly to complete and/or implement.
61–70	The evaluation will be completed and/or implemented only with considerable difficulty.
71–80	The difficulties in evaluation and/or implementation will be such that the evaluation should not be undertaken, unless it is essential to the resource allocation process.

Time
(the estimated length of time, in staff months, to complete an evaluation)

1	1 to 3 months
2	4 to 6 months
3	7 to 9 months
4	10 to 12 months
5	over 12 months

Cost of Materials
(the estimated costs, other than staffing, involved in the completion of an evaluation)

1	$0 to $5,000
2	$5,001 to $10,000
3	$10,001 to $15,000
4	$15,001 to $25,000
5	over $25,000

Staffing Costs
(personnel, both permanent and temporary, associated with an evaluation)

1	$0 to $15,000
2	$15,001 to $30,000
3	$30,001 to $45,000
4	$45,001 to $60,000
5	over $60,000

Exhibit 1. *(continued)*

Resistance
(the estimated degree of potential or likely opposition that evaluated units will manifest before, during, and after an evaluation)

2	The evaluated units buy into the evaluation and will make positive inputs into the methodology.
4	The evaluated units partially buy into the evaluation but will not contribute to the process.
6	The evaluated units accept the evaluation.
8	The evaluated units are somewhat resistant to the evaluation.
10	The evaluated units are strongly opposed to the evaluation.

Purpose
(how well the goals, objectives, and performance criteria of the program to be evaluated are laid out)

1	Goals and objectives are well defined, and measurement criteria are appropriate and are utilized.
2	Goals and objectives are defined; measurement criteria are appropriate but are not utilized.
3	Goals, objectives, and measurement criteria are partially defined; or goals and objectives are well defined, but measurement criteria are missing or inappropriate.
4	Goals or objectives or measurement criteria are missing.
5	Goals, objectives, and measurement criteria are missing.

Maturity
(the reasonableness in evaluating a program in terms of its maturity)

1	The program is well established (more than five years old) and not in a state of flux.
2	The program is well established but has undergone minor changes.
3	The program has been in existence for a relatively short period of time (two to five years) but is stable.
4	The program has been in existence for only one to two years.
5	The program is less than one year old.

Definition
(the clarity of the design, function, and structure of the program)

1	The program is well defined, the components are easily identifiable, and its structure is clearly laid out.
2	The program is defined, though some components are difficult to isolate; the structure is clear.
3	The program is partially defined; many components and the structure are not easily identifiable.
4	The program, its components, and structure are poorly defined.
5	The program, its components, and structure are undefined.

Exhibit 1. *(continued)*

Validity
(the ability to measure program accomplishments against goals and objectives)

1	The program results are easily quantifiable and accurately measure program efficiency and/or effectiveness.
2	The program results are easily quantifiable but are only partially accurate as measurement criteria.
3	The program results can be quantified with some difficulty; measurement is partially accurate.
4	The program results must be measured in large part subjectively with limited quantifiable data.
5	Data cannot be quantified or are not available.

Reliability
(the ability to obtain consistent results when measuring program performance)

1	Results will consistently be the same.
2	Results will usually be the same; some minor variation should be anticipated.
3	Results will often be the same; variations may occur and results should be carefully cross-checked.
4	Results will be inconsistent; substantial variations may occur, and impacting variables must be isolated.
5	Results will be subjective and largely unreliable because of the lack of quantifiable data.

Constraints
(potential barriers—administrative, political [internal or external] and legal—to obtaining data or implementing recommendations)

A. Administrative (constraints growing out of agency policy or process)

2	There are no administrative constraints to the evaluation.
4	Administrative constraints are relatively minor; impacting variables must be isolated.
6	Administrative constraints exist that could delay or partially limit the effectiveness of the evaluation.
8	Substantial administrative constraints exist that will weaken the effectiveness of the evaluation.
10	Administrative constraints will severely hamper the evaluation or implementation of evaluation recommendations.

B. Political (constraints growing out of the dynamics of the agency itself or its governing forces)

2	There are no political constraints to the evaluation.
4	Political constraints are relatively minor.
6	Political constraints exist that could delay or partially limit the effectiveness of the evaluation.

Exhibit 1. *(continued)*

8	Substantial political constraints exist that will weaken the effectiveness of the evaluation.
10	Political constraints will severely hamper the evaluation or implementation of evaluation recommendations.

C. Legal (constraints or limitations imposed by law on the availability of data, accessibility of program managers, or ability to implement recommendations)

2	There are no legal constraints to the evaluation.
4	Legal constraints are relatively minor.
6	Legal constraints exist that could delay or partially limit the effectiveness of the evaluation.
8	Substantial administrative constraints exist that will weaken the effectiveness of the evaluation.
10	Administrative constraints will severely hamper the evaluation or implementation of evaluation recommendations.

Figure 2. Criteria for Prioritizing Topics

CRITERIA	A	B	C	D	E	F
Evaluation Interest (1-5 Points)						
Organizational Impact (1-5 Points)						
Financial Impact (1-5 Points)						
Operational Budget (1-5 Points)						
Immediacy (1-5 Points)						
Difficulty (From Figure 1) (1-5 Points)						
Total Rating Points (6-30)						

Exhibit 2. Rating Scales for Prioritization Criteria

1. *Executive Interest*—What is the perceived value of the program from management's perspective?
   a. A sense of urgency has been expressed.
   b. A very high level of concern has been expressed.
   c. Some concern has been expressed.
   d. No concern has been expressed.
   e. The topic has been categorized as a low priority.

2. *Organizational Impact*—How does the program affect the organization as a whole?
   a. Cuts across all departments
   b. Cuts across most departments
   c. Cuts across about half the departments
   d. Impacts on several departments
   e. Impacts only one or two departments

3. *Financial Impact*—What is the estimated cost of the program?
   a. Resource commitments/revenues are in excess of $50 million.
   b. Resource commitments/revenues are between $41 and $50 million.
   c. Resource commmitments/revenues are between $26 and $40 million.
   d. Resource commitments/revenues are between $11 and $25 million.
   e. Resource commitments/revenues are less than $10 million.

4. *Operational Impact*—To what extent would modifications in the program to be evaluated affect the organization?
   a. Change to the program would have substantial impact on agencywide operations.
   b. Change to the program would have a substantial impact on a limited basis within the agency.
   c. Change to the program would have minor impact on an agencywide basis.
   d. Change to the program would have minor impact on a limited basis within the agency.
   e. Change to the program would have little or no operational impact.

5. *Immediacy*—How quickly does the organization need the evaluation data?
   a. Resolution of program issues is necessary as soon as possible.
   b. Resolution of program issues is necessary within six months.
   c. Resolution of program issues is necessary within one year.
   d. Resolution of program issues is a low-priority item.
   e. No issues have as yet been identified but the program is due to be evaluated.

6. *Difficulty of Evaluation*—According to the difficulty assessment as documented in Figure 1, is the evaluation reasonable?

1	Criteria Total—	16–30
2		31–45
3		46–60
4		61–70
5		71–80

Note: If total is more than 71, the evaluation will be very difficult and typically should not be undertaken.

be sensitive to opportunities that may exist, as well as the danger of wasting resources. The environment—both internal and external—political implications, and human resource impact are all pieces of the equation that weighs the advantages and disadvantages of alternatives. The ultimate benefit, which is now always measured in terms of cost—as well as the immediate bottom line—should be considered of equal importance. The second concept is the realization that although the ideal alternative is an admirable pursuit, it can well be a fruitless one. The best alternative is one that addresses successfully the main concerns providing impetus to the request for the evaluation and hence its utility. This can often be arrived at without spending an enormous amount of time locating missing pieces of information that do not contribute substantially to completion of the review. This is not to condone incomplete staff work but to recognize that the value of missing variables must be assessed in terms of worth to the final product and staff time expended.

In the corporate or quasi-corporate environment, these considerations are essential to enhance the credibility and utilization of program review as both an objective and positive organization change agent, to obtain the commitment of decision makers, and to provide support for the practice of other ongoing and future evaluation work. Utilization of the framework presented can assist program evaluators and staff in arriving at a decision concerning which evaluations should be conducted. This will help ensure the achievement of the organization's goals.

Daniel B. Muscatello is administrator for program review and evaluation for the Port Authority of New York and New Jersey. His interests focus on large-scale program evaluations conducted within complex organizations and factors that contribute to their utilization by program staff and organization management.

*This chapter addresses the problems that physicians, hospital
administrators, and patients have in understanding and
supporting the use of evaluation in the delivery of health
care services. Strategies designed to gain greater acceptance
of evaluation from these client groups are presented.*

The Impact of Major Consumer Groups on Health Care Evaluation

Tara D. Knott

In no field is evaluation more potentially valuable than in health care;
however, evaluation's acceptance is far from complete. It is the responsibility of those of us who practice in this area to increase this acceptance
by providing the best work possible and by continually identifying and
creating opportunities for evaluation in health care. Such vigilance and
dedication to both evaluation and the improvement of health care should
result in the increased utilization of evaluation in the health care delivery
system.

With the increased attention given to accountability in health care by
both the public and private sectors and the popular move toward more
patient involvement in the delivery of health care services, evaluation is
becoming increasingly important in ensuring quality services in the
health care delivery system. Unfortunately, the utilization of evaluation
in health care often receives a relatively low priority by those who have
the responsibility and authority to fund, instigate, and use evaluation
studies.

This chapter describes the three major consumer groups that would
benefit most from health care evaluation. The problems each group has

J. A. McLaughlin, L. J. Weber, R. W. Covert, and R. B. Ingle (eds.). *Evaluation Utilization.*
New Directions for Program Evaluation, no. 39. San Francisco: Jossey-Bass, Fall 1988.

in understanding and supporting the use of evaluation in the delivery of health care services is also addressed. By overtly and realistically addressing the concerns of each of these three consumer groups, the opportunities for evaluation and its use in health care settings can hopefully be improved. Helping health care deliverers maintain and increase the quality of patient care is also a goal.

Context Dependency

The practice of evaluation is clearly influenced by the dual contexts in which health care exists. In fact, utilization of evaluation in health care will only be increased when evaluators appreciate the uniqueness and duality of these contexts.

Health care is big business and must be treated as such. Issues such as timeliness of information and attention to the bottom line are crucial in today's medical market place. However, health care remains dedicated to the promotion of the public good. Information traditionally associated with social programming, such as equal availability, justice, and quality of services, must also be made available to decision makers.

Evaluators must familiarize themselves with both of these contexts so they can identify and resolve those problems within each context that militate against the use of evaluation in the field as a whole.

Major Consumer Groups

Scriven (1981) instructs us that consumers of an evaluand include groups of people who are directly and indirectly affected—that is, all of the audiences of an evaluand are consumers thereof. This concept is exemplified in health care wherein the evaluand often directly affects not only patients but has an important indirect effect on physicians and hospital administrators as well.

There are three major consumer groups having information needs that must be met by those who conduct evaluations in health care settings. The provision of health care services is dominated by two of these groups: physicians and hospital administrators. Each of these groups of professionals has specific but vastly disparate expectations for health care programs. This is unfortunate because these professionals are the ultimate decision makers about health care programming and the disbursement of health care funds. The third consumer group for health care services is the patients. This target group of consumers, for whom health care services are eventually intended, have their own needs, concerns, and expectations about the delivery and effectiveness of health care.

Each of these major groups has very different expectations concerning health care. These expectations have a direct impact on whether or not an evaluation is accepted, how it is designed, whether or not it is used, and how it is used. By examining each of these groups' concerns and expectations about health care evaluation, evaluators will be in a better position to sensitively and realistically approach health care professionals with ideas for needed studies. Evaluators can then design those studies for maximum usefulness.

Physicians

In order to understand this group's concerns about and problems with evaluation, evaluators must understand a few things about physicians and the context in which they train and practice. Physicians are typically highly respected and well-paid professionals who have trained diligently and who sincerely care about their patients and their health concerns. Many of these same good doctors are extremely autocratic with regard to decision making. Unfortunately, this autocratic attitude is often the result of medical training and the traditional practice of medicine in which physicians are treated by support staff and patients as larger than life (Illich, 1976). This posture, however understandable, can be highly problematic for health care evaluators. Physicians, who rightfully make independent clinical decisions about patient care on a daily basis, are also inclined to make independent decisions about all health-related matters. This includes whether or not a treatment program is evaluated, how it is evaluated, and by whom. Physician autocracy is the first of several problems physicians typically present to evaluators.

Even when a physician is convinced that a health care program should be evaluated, he or she may believe that "only a physician can evaluate another physician." This belief extends to the treatment provided or training received by physicians. Unfortunately, this attitude is rather pervasive in the medical community (Lasswell and Smith, 1987). This attitude is probably a result of traditional physician training and the closed nature of the medical community. Although somewhat understandable, this antiquated attitude is clearly a major context-dependent problem for evaluators in health care settings.

The desire of the medical community to protect its own (that is, physicians' desire to maintain the right to decide whether or not a physician found to be incompetent can continue to practice) is widely recognized. While this is not the forum to debate that issue, the extension of this attitude to include the perceived protection of entire treatment programs is the focus here, since the extension of this attitude is problematic for evaluators. Many physicians appear to have difficulty separating the worker from the work. They fail to understand that a treatment program can be minimally effective even though the physicians who deliver the treatment may be highly competent and conscientious.

Further, a physician who designs or is heavily involved in the implementation of a treatment program has, as do other program developers, a personal stake in the success of the program. This is also understandable and desirable. However, if the same physician is responsible for deciding whether or not the program will undergo a systematic evaluation to determine future funding, such a situation is clearly not desirable. In such a case, the physician's stake in the program may effectively obviate any attempt to demonstrate the actual program effectiveness or lack thereof. If the program is evaluated, this may cause the physician to view the results from a biased perspective.

Still another problem physicians often have with health care evaluation is the fact that their training typically includes a plethora of basic experimental studies. For example, physicians are well aware that the law requires that all new drugs be subjected to classic double blind testing before they are allowed to be used in this country. While this allegiance by many physicians to experimental protocol is understandable by virtue of their training, it represents a problem for health care evaluators, who cannot always mount experimental or quasi-experimental studies. Even when a "nonscientific" approach is accepted, physicians and other health care professionals tend to label the resultant information as anecdotal and relatively inconsequential (O'Donnel, 1986). Evaluation is seldom valued for its own uses but instead is considered a first step toward a "real, scientific" study.

As in all areas of evaluation, there is also a realistic concern among physicians that evaluation will take too much staff time and effort. The delivery of health care services is the prime concern of physicians, and they passionately argue against most activities that interfere with such delivery. While this sentiment is highly appropriate, evaluators must convince physicians that it is equally as important to ensure that those health care services that are delivered are maximally effective and available to all who need them.

Thus the major problems evaluators often have in their negotiations with physicians are

1. The medical community is relatively closed, and many physicians do not welcome outsiders.
2. Many physicians are accustomed to autocratic decision making about individual patient treatment and tend to extend this attitude to treatment programs as well.
3. Physicians, like other program instigators, have a high personal and professional stake in their treatment programs and in the delivery of health care services per se.
4. Physicians' training typically includes a plethora of strictly controlled, experimental studies. Therefore, physicians may not easily accept nonexperimental approaches.

5. Physicians rightfully believe that the delivery of health care is their primary concern and may perceive evaluation as an unnecessary nuisance.

Problem-Solving Approaches for Physicians

Recall the first problem identified for physicians: the closed nature of the medical community. Whether just or not, many physicians prefer to work with other physicians and are more accepting of their ideas than they are of those of nonphysicians. The problem becomes how does a nonphysician evaluator make an initial and acceptable contact with a medical doctor? There are several ways.

If there is a medical school in the evaluator's vicinity, this is a good place to begin to develop a relationship with physicians. Because physicians who are also faculty members are already engaged in an educational endeavor, they must be somewhat more accepting of educators and other nonphysician professionals who are instrumental in training young doctors. An entré via this route is certainly worth a try. Evaluators can approach the heads of various medical school departments to find out what sorts of evaluation activities are currently underway in their departments. They then can offer to assist with these efforts. An evaluator might also offer to conduct a workshop on evaluation uses at a departmental meeting. This approach allows evaluators a kind of reverse "guilt by association"—that is, a doctor may reason that if an evaluator is acceptable to the medical school and department chair, then it might not hurt to listen to his or her ideas.

A second way to approach physicians is to find out what sorts of treatment regimens interest them. Involve the client in the evaluation. For example, if you know a physician has a special interest in the fetal alcoholism syndrome (FAS), you might contact him or her to ascertain whether or not the FAS programs with which he or she is involved have been evaluated. This might result in an appointment to discuss such a study with the physician and gives the evaluator an opportunity to convince the physician that the evaluator not only has the methodological skills required but also can obtain the field expertise that will be needed.

The closely related problem of physician autocracy regarding decision making, which is the most elusive of those physician-related problems identified earlier in the chapter, can also be managed via the above approaches. However, evaluators should remember that many physicians expect to make the final decision regarding health care—whether it is for an individual or a program. It is the evaluator's job to help the physician have as much useful information as possible so that the decision is a good one.

Evaluators must also be prepared to discuss the second concern previously mentioned in connection with physicians, namely, the ownership most physicians feel toward their programs. The evaluator should be able to respond to questions such as "what if 'my' program is found to be ineffective?" In these situations, it becomes the evaluator's job to explain that because most treatment programs have benefited from excellent planning and are typically designed specifically to meet a set of identified patient needs, few programs are found to be totally ineffective. A discussion of these kinds of issues will help convince physicians that the evaluator is sensitive to their concerns and will work with them to ensure that the delivery of health care services is as good as possible.

The evaluator might also attempt to draw physicians into a discussion of ways in which they think the program might be improved. This would provide an opportunity to discuss formative evaluation and to explain how evaluation can systematically guide decision makers to the most feasible and productive program improvements. Physicians often begin to support evaluation when they perceive it as a method by which they can obtain "hard" data with which to convince funding sources such as hospital administrators that their program should be continued or expanded. Physicians must be convinced that evaluation is not only nonthreatening but will actually be useful to them.

With regard to the problem of rigid evaluation design, physicians will often question the evaluator about the inclusion of a control group or some other methodological issue arising from the physician's scientific training. The evaluator should be prepared for this concern and might consider a brief but pointed discussion of the intended uses of the evaluation results and how these uses often differ from the intended uses of experimental and quasi-experimental designs. The evaluator might explain that while basic, experimental research paradigms typically test various hypotheses, evaluations are designed to determine value. The physician should be assured that although a strict research paradigm may be the ideal situation, such an approach is typically impossible in health care programming. The evaluator could then continue to explain that the types and level of information collected via the evaluation will suffice for the decision-making needs of most program managers. For example, the delivery system of a nutrition program supplying milk for underprivileged infants might be improved based on the "nonscientific" evaluation finding that most potential clients cannot find transportation to the poorly located program. Few physicians would question the value of knowing this information simply because a nonexperimental design was used to collect it. Physicians certainly understand the ethics and reasoning behind design problems; however, they may not be accustomed to thinking about more practical evaluation-specific design problems. In fact, to many physicians, evaluation and research are synonymous.

Another major concern most physicians share is whether the evaluation will interfere with the delivery of health care services. They do not want evaluators peeking over their staffs' and patients' shoulders and generally disrupting treatment. To address this realistic concern, the evaluator should be prepared to familiarize physicians with typical evaluation approaches. Several tentative approaches might be presented in sufficient detail so that the physicians are comfortable about what to expect from the evaluators. Physicians will want to know some specifics, such as how many evaluators will be on site, how they will be trained, how they will interact with the staff and patients, and so on. The evaluator in this situation should have a lot of design ideas to present and should be flexible and responsive to the physician's concerns and suggestions. Specific ways in which the final information might be used should also be given so that physicians can decide whether or not the evaluation results will be worth the inconvenience of the study. Evaluators should be extremely familiar with the federal confidentiality laws and regulations and should ideally introduce a discussion of the ways in which patient confidentiality will be guarded.

Finally, it is important for the evaluator to learn the language of the physician. While no one expects evaluators to be conversant in the technical jargon of the field, it is imperative that they know a DRG from a DSM III.

These are some ways in which the concerns of physicians about evaluation might be handled. The major caveat in dealing with physicians, as with other professionals, is to solicit their input and to sincerely listen to their ideas. In fact, physicians, like other program managers, can often help the evaluator identify points that might have otherwise been inadvertently ignored. Further, since they are trained scientists, they can also assist a great deal with the design per se. Additionally, they know the literature and may also know about other programs attempting to do the same thing as the program about to be evaluated. Such inside information is, of course, extremely helpful for evaluation planning. Hopefully, the foregoing suggestions will help the evaluator convince the physician that his or her support for a formal evaluation will be of use in obtaining needed information.

Hospital Administrators

The second powerful health care group that can support or undermine the practice of evaluation is hospital administrators. These persons, who are often trained in business schools or departments of public health, are essentially business people who literally hold the purse strings for hospital budgets. Since many treatment programs occur in hospital settings, administrators must be convinced that evaluation can be used as an effective means of improving health care administration.

Because they are responsible for all budget expenditures, administrators approach evaluation as one of a variety of important projects that require resources from their limited pool of funds. In this evaluator's experience, administrators often assign evaluation a low priority when compared to, say, a new x-ray suite or some other highly tangible and visible hospital need.

Another problem for hospital administrators is that the term *evaluation* is too closely associated with the activities of oversight agencies such as the Joint Commission for the Accreditation of Hospitals (JCAH), which sometimes appears to focus more on what is wrong than what is right. In addition, such evaluation activities typically consume a great deal of staff time and effort and are seldom used for anything other than passing the survey. In light of these experiences, it is not surprising that administrators might view evaluation with some disdain.

It should also be noted that some administrators are not amenable to having their programs evaluated because they fear competitive hospitals may somehow find out the results and benefit from their shortcomings. Although the concept of overt marketing is relatively new in health care, the field is highly competitive. Every hospital wants and claims to be the best. The fact that these claims are often based on wishful thinking and not demonstrated effectiveness seems to be overlooked by administrators, marketers, and often the patients themselves.

Further, administrators do not want to irritate their consumers—either patients or physicians. Many administrators persist in believing that evaluation will somehow violate their patients' right to privacy. They are also acutely aware that some patients file lawsuits over issues of violated privacy rights. This is certainly a right of patients and a crucial concern for all health care evaluators. It can be well handled by assuring the administrator that an experienced evaluator is familiar with the applicable laws and regulations.

Finally, administrators are loath to alienate physicians who practice at their facilities. The relationship between physicians and administrators is often already strained, and administrators are not usually willing to support an evaluation that further may test that relationship. The major reasons that physicians are uncomfortable with evaluation have already been discussed and are certainly well known to administrators, who must depend on these physicians to staff their hospitals. Physician concerns about evaluation, then, also become the concerns of the administrators, who must ensure that their hospitals have adequate medical staff complements. Further, it is these physicians who are requesting the same monies—monies that could fund an evaluation—for much-needed staff and equipment. Physicians have fiscal needs and wants that compete with evaluation, and the administrator is placed in the position of choosing between them.

Administrators, because of the business context in which they exist, present their own set of problems to evaluators. These problems include the following:

- Administrators are responsible for limited resource pools, and evaluation is typically not a high priority.
- Administrators' typical experience with evaluation leads them to believe that it is a waste of time.
- Administrators do not want to lose their competitive edge because of an evaluation that found negative results and that somehow became public knowledge.
- Administrators want to protect their patients' privacy and avoid potentially litigious situations.
- Administrators do not want to strain their already tenuous relationship with physicians.

Problem-Solving Approaches for Administrators

In part because evaluation is relatively new to the health care scene, it is typically not the highest priority for health care administrators. As previously discussed, administrators must also attempt to provide everything for everybody—equipment, materials, and services needed by the physicians, nursing staff, dietary staff, maintenance, and so on—from the same limited pool of resources. With the heads of these services each clamoring for funding, the administrator's position is difficult indeed. Evaluators must not only be sensitive to the demands placed on hospital administration, they also must be prepared to convince administrators that evaluation is as, or more, important than the other demands being placed on the finite resource pool. In order to accomplish this, the evaluator must first believe that the proposed study will benefit the hospital in some tangible way and must be prepared to give evidence thereof. For example, if an evaluator believes that the superiority of a particular treatment regime can be demonstrated, he or she might develop a proposal for the administrator, stating the specific ways in which treatment could be improved, costs reduced, or both. This is the sort of information that impresses administrators and, for that matter, most decision makers.

The second problem is the fact that many administrators associate the process of evaluation with the often tedious and endless surveys that hospitals must periodically pass. These surveys, while certainly important to ensure adequate patient care, are typically not shining examples of state-of-the-art evaluation. These surveys can best be described as single-shot, on-site observations by a team of surveyors and evaluators who are armed with volumes of standards—some of which may not have been scrutinized, let alone changed, for decades. (This situation has recently begun to change as oversight agencies such as the JCAH have begun to appoint self-study groups to review the standards in several services, for example, medical surgery.) Hospitals undergoing such surveys must provide detailed manuals of the goals and objectives for each department and documentation that they were met. While this survey method may be helpful, evaluatively, to the hospital's self-study, it is not helpful in convincing administrators that evaluation is as useful as, for instance, an x-ray machine. Evaluators have the job of persuading administrators that a well-designed evaluation requires less work from hospital staff and is more useful for decision making than a typical survey.

It should also be noted that evaluators can use the mandated survey process to help convince administrators that state-of-the-art evaluation is a useful process. For example, many of the standards from the JCAH, such as those for quality assurance, require evaluation. Evaluators can help administrators understand that the entire survey process can be more than "pencil titration" if treated from an overall evaluation perspective. After all, the surveys by the JCAH, Medicare/Medicaid, and others are evaluation activities; however, in most hospitals these evaluations tend to be disjointed and unrelated. Administrators are always searching for ways to reduce the staffs' work load and simultaneously maintain quality of patient care. This is a glowing opportunity for evaluators to "show their stuff."

A third problem is that some administrators, like other program directors, are convinced that the results of any evaluation, especially negative ones, will be made public knowledge. Even though most administrators realize intellectually that this is seldom the case, the residual fears about public failure surface when an evaluation is proposed. In the case of hospital administrators, these fears are somewhat substantiated, since a poor evaluation made public could easily result in a business catastrophe, with patients looking elsewhere for treatment. However, especially in the past decade, businesses as well as individual patients have begun to demand that hospitals provide them with information about the costs and, sometimes, the effects of treatment. It is our job as evaluators to convince administrators that we can assist them in determining these costs and effects without divulging corporate secrets or "airing dirty linen."

Another genuine concern of administrators is the dim view that patients may take of evaluation, since many perceive it as a threat to their privacy. Because the administrator is ultimately responsible, any potentially uncomfortable and possibly litigious situation is carefully considered. It is the responsibility of the evaluator to convince the administrator that the evaluator is familiar with all relevant federal and other laws and regulations and that they will be meticulously followed. In order to do this, evaluators must become familiar with these laws and be conversant about the methods in which the laws will be followed.

The final problem administrators often have with evaluation is that they must maintain good relationships with their facility's physicians. This is sometimes difficult due, in part, to the physician-related problems already discussed. Therefore, even if an administrator is convinced that an outcome study for premature babies is an excellent idea, he or she must convince the obstetricians and pediatricians. Since administrators, perhaps rightfully, do not want to introduce controversy where none exists, it will be up to the evaluator to discover ways to ensure that the physicians support the evaluation.

As discussed in the section on problem-solving approaches for physicians, the evaluator's mastery of the language used in health care settings is important. Administrators and physicians speak much the same language, and evaluators who choose to work in this arena must familiarize themselves with it to obtain maximal effectiveness.

Patients

The last important group of health care consumers is the patients. In this evaluator's experience, patients' major concerns about evaluation are twofold: they are concerned about the confidentiality of any information provided and about the intended uses of that information.

For fear of reprisal, no patient wants to make negative remarks about a physician or hospital and then be again in a position to require medical assistance from that source. Patients who must depend on public health care programs may be concerned about negative consequences from health care staff, whom they perceive as their only medical resource. These patients, in particular, may be resistant to any attempt to obtain evaluation information from them.

Patients in both private and public programs share a common concern about the possibility of their medical information becoming public knowledge. For example, some employers may look with disfavor on an employee who enters treatment for an emotional problem. Or patients with certain types of problems, such as AIDS, may risk personal retribution from an ill-informed society. The unauthorized disclosure of such information is therefore personally dangerous, and evaluators must give assurance to patients and inform them that they are well aware of this situation and forbidden by law to share information with anyone without a signed consent.

Further, patients are by definition ill and therefore may not feel well enough to answer questions about their care. They may decline participation on this basis. Additionally, patients may not feel competent to make comments about health care practices that they only minimally understand.

Finally, most patients do not understand the purposes for which an evaluation is conducted. Hospitalized patients are asked to sign releases for many things, such as the administration of anesthesia. This multitude of requests, coupled with the ever-increasing awareness of potentially dangerous or litigious situations, often causes patients to be wary of all requests for their signature on forms they sometimes only marginally understand.

There are, then, several evaluation problems presented by patients as a group.

- Patients typically do not understand the purposes of an evaluation.
- Patients are concerned about the confidentiality of medical and personal information.
- Patients fear reprisal from the health care system if negative remarks are made.
- Patients may be too ill to cooperate with evaluation.
- Patients may be too poorly educated regarding health care procedures to participate in the evaluation.

Problem-Solving Approaches for Patients

After an evaluator has convinced the physician or the hospital administrator that an evaluation is a worthwhile endeavor, there is one remaining group whose concerns must be addressed: the patients. Although much of the task of convincing patients to participate is handled by physicians and administrators, it is the patients who ultimately make or break the evaluation, since they have the legal right to refuse to participate.

As previously mentioned, patients are legally, as well as morally, entitled to privacy. Their health-related information is theirs alone unless they grant permission for it to be used. Health care evaluators should continually bear this in mind. Obviously, in order to comply with the federal laws pertaining to patient confidentiality, the health care evaluator should ascertain which laws are applicable and learn them. It is also helpful to retain a lawyer who is well versed in this area of the law. Be forewarned that most lawyers are not. Lawyers who work with the public sector are often familiar with these laws or can recommend a colleague who is. Hospital attorneys must, of course, be cognizant of these laws. Once the evaluator knows the laws and has access to someone who can interpret them and give them advice for specific situations, he or she is ready to design the confidentiality forms to be used by the patients.

The next step is obtaining the patient's written consent. This is sometimes not very easy. I have found that it is often the staff member who initially presents and explains the confidentiality form who is responsible for patient cooperation or lack thereof. A thorough in-service training session, in which the design is explained and the reasons for the study reviewed with the staff, is a good approach to this problem.

If, however, the evaluator must personally obtain the patients' consent, he or she must be prepared to explain the evaluation to the patients in understandable terms so that the intended uses of the information are entirely clear. Most patients will agree to participate in an evaluation if they are convinced that the information will only be used by the evaluator to help improve the program or document its effectiveness. The evaluator must also make it clear that no individual information will be used in any report. Mental health patients and patients who have diseases that may result in some public discrimination especially must be convinced that no one except the evaluator will have access to their information. Health care evaluators must remain aware of the patients' desires and legal rights to refuse to participate in an evaluation.

A second problem that patients have with evaluation is their fear of reprisal from the health care system. Although it would appear that this is more of a problem in the public sector, it is my experience that those in the private health care system also have this apprehension. Some patients and their families believe that if they make a negative remark about a particular physician or nurse, that person will revenge themselves by not providing adequate care in the future. Although this fear is probably unfounded, it can serve as a powerful deterrent to patient involvement. Again, if the evaluator can include the health care providers in every step of the evaluation, they may be willing to help convince patients that this fear is unfounded. Certainly, the evaluator should take steps to ensure that the staff is aware of the evaluation and its purposes so that they are comfortable with explaining it to the patients.

Finally, it should be noted that patients are, by definition, ill and not at their best. Simple common sense and courtesy should lead an evaluator to request a patient's approval to participate when the patient is as comfortable as possible and pain free. Patient advocacy groups might be asked to intervene in situations in which a patient is too ill to personally grant consent. It has been my experience that admission and discharge are two good times to request this permission; however, with internal studies, meal times and bedtime medicine rounds are also typically successful.

Conclusion

This chapter has identified the three major consumer groups for health care evaluation and has discussed several problems specific to each. Each of these groups represents a different facet of health care: hospital administrators reflect health care as big business, patients reflect health care as the promotion of social good, and physicians have allegiances to both of these groups as well as to their guild of scientists-physicians.

For business, the information needs are action oriented. That is, of primary importance to evaluators are the timeliness and usefulness of information that they can deliver to decision makers for more effective program management and decisive action.

For health care as social programming, the information needs of most importance concern the more traditional evaluation roles of providing information and making recommendations for the continual improvement of the system. It is this sort of information that is typically required and understood by physicians and patient advocates.

Each of these facets combines to comprise the complicated context in which health care services are delivered. Harshbarger (1984) has emphasized that the lines between the public and private sectors are fading and that evaluators must seriously reconsider their traditional roles in this changing environment. As health care evaluators, we must certainly reconsider our traditional roles and learn to solve the evaluation problems presented by each of the consumer groups comprising the complicated, but rewarding, field of medicine.

References

Harshbarger, D. "Value Added to the Evaluator." *Evaluation News*, 1984, *5* (1), 20–32.

Illich, I. *Medical Nemesis: The Expropriation of Health.* New York: Pantheon Books, 1976.

Lasswell, A., and Smith, S. R. "Attitudes of Medical Students and Faculty Members Toward Non-Physician Faculty Members." *Journal of Medical Education*, 1987, *62*, 509–511.

O'Donnel, M. "Publisher's Welcome." *American Journal of Health Promotion*, 1986, *1* (1), 1–3.

Scriven, M. *Evaluation Thesaurus.* Pt. Reyes, Calif.: Edgepress, 1981.

Tara D. Knott is president of Evaluation Resources Incorporated, an evaluation firm. Her primary interest is to increase the visibility and use of evaluation in both the public and private sectors.

*Just as we expend effort to acquire resources to design and
conduct effective evaluations, so should our energies be directed
at ensuring that evaluations will be used. Suggestions for
enhancing the use of evaluation studies are the major focus
of this chapter.*

Getting the System
to Respond to
Evaluation Findings

Carol T. Mowbray

Taking my first evaluation job after graduate school in psychology, I
was quite interested in the emerging literature on the utilization of
evaluation results. I was fascinated by the fact that there might even be
an issue over evaluation results *not* being used to make decisions. On
review of the research and writings available at the time (circa 1975), I
discovered that the explanations for nonutilization could be grouped
into two simple categories: blame the evaluator and blame the decision
maker (see Exhibit 1).

Later, while working as an evaluator for a state government, I soon
realized that the explanations in Exhibit 1 were not sufficient to fully
understand the complexity of the decision-making process at the state
level and the ways evaluation could have more of an impact. Fortunately, other literature added to my knowledge. Rich (1975) differentiated
between *instrumental uses* of evaluation findings (for example, specific
fact inputs used in documentable ways to answer specific questions)
versus *conceptual uses* (for example, influencing a policymaker's thinking about an issue but not necessarily resulting in a documentable use
of specific information). While instrumental uses of evaluation results

J. A. McLaughlin, L. J. Weber, R. W. Covert, and R. B. Ingle (eds.). *Evaluation Utilization.*
New Directions for Program Evaluation, no. 39. San Francisco: Jossey-Bass, Fall 1988.

Exhibit 1. Explanations for Nonutilization of Evaluation Results

Blame the Evaluator

1. The results were not presented appropriately:
   - Not enough visuals (bar graphs or pie charts)
   - Too technical.
2. The results were not useful:
   - Study too abstract or esoteric
   - Study not relevant
   - Results not timely.

Blame the Decision Maker

1. The decision makers were not involved in advance and lacked interest.
2. Decision makers were not interested in facts:
   - Undue influence by political pressures or funding issues
   - Too absorbed in day-to-day operations
   - Inattention to long-range, data-based decision making.
3. Decision makers want a "quick fix."
4. Decision makers do not know what they want.

may be relatively rare, conceptual uses can have a long-term and significant impact on policy decisions, how problems are defined, and in setting overall policy directions that are compatible with accumulated knowledge.

Another person who influenced my thinking was Nagel (1983), who asserted that utilization does occur more than suggested by earlier literature. This fact is not recognized by evaluators because their expectations may be too high and the time frames used to track evaluation utilization too short. According to Nagel, most evaluators want their findings to "single-handedly" cause a 180-degree reversal in the way an agency is heading. This rarely occurs—no matter how competent the evaluator, how valued the study, or how dramatic the results. Nagel has indicated that a more common use of an evaluation study is to solidify a direction in which an agency is already heading or to raise questions that might modify an established course.

Finally, Chelimsky (1986, 1987) has examined much of the early work on nonutilization and added an understanding of the political and decision-making process. Chelimsky (1986) has pointed out that in understanding evaluation utilization, "we are dealing with a process of continual translation for which the evaluator must assume a major share of the responsibility" (p. 9). A five-stage continuum by which this process takes place was set forth by Chelimsky.

For the present discussion on utilization of evaluation results in mental health at the state level, I will build on Chelimsky's framework, add two stages of my own, and provide clarification and examples from personal experience. My presentation will outline some issues and choices that will enable evaluators to maximize utilization. Some of these activities may require evaluators to assume roles they may not normally want. Also, some evaluators may prefer to have their reports sit on shelves or have them published in little-read journals rather than take on the challenge imposed by a more active involvement in politics, decision making, and system operations.

Background

Before proceeding to outline the steps I feel are necessary to maximize the utilization of evaluations, I should describe the responsibilities of the research and evaluation division in the Michigan Department of Mental Health. At the division we have three major functions:

1. Carrying out and/or overseeing the evaluation of demonstration projects, which include such diverse areas as outreach programs to the mentally ill, homeless, and adolescent sex offenders. Evaluation methods vary from basic process approaches to a true experiment. Based on our findings, recommendations are made about whether programs should be continued, expanded, replicated, modified, or terminated.

2. Providing funding to specified evaluation studies under contract and monitoring performance. For specific topical areas, we develop RFPs (requests for proposals), select the best proposals, negotiate contracts, monitor evaluation efforts, provide technical assistance and support, evaluate the adequacy of final reports, request changes, and disseminate results as appropriate.

3. Conducting evaluation studies directly with a small group of in-house evaluation specialists. Topics may be specified by the director or other executive staff or requested by the legislature or outside research grantors (such as the National Institute of Mental Health or Office of Human Development Services).

Steps in Maximizing Utilization

The six steps I have identified as necessary for maximizing utilization follow
1. Marketing evaluation as a worthwhile service
2. Developing and focusing policy questions (Chelimsky's step 1)
3. Planning and designing the evaluation (Chelimsky's step 2)
4. Conducting the evaluation (Chelimsky's step 3)
5. Translating findings (Chelimsky's step 4)
6. Making people pay attention to evaluation results.
Step 4, of course, is what evaluators are trained to do. Steps 3 and 5 have been addressed through the substantial literature on utilization. Steps 1, 2, and 6 are those for which most evaluators are unprepared and untrained, and that evaluators are perhaps unwilling to assume.

Step 1. Marketing Evaluation as a Worthwhile Service. Marketing is that change in executives' conceptual framework (Rich, 1975) such that every time they are involved in an upcoming major decision, they call on an evaluator to gather and present relevant information about the issue. When they embark on a new service program or a new funding initiative, they set aside resources for an evaluation component that can be adequately conducted. Chelimsky does not include this step in her system. Perhaps it is because the federal government has reached the point of sophistication where evaluation is expected and its "use is the rule, not the exception" (Chelimsky, 1986, p. 16). However, for most evaluators in state and local agencies, this is not so.

How is marketing accomplished? It is a long-term process and results from continually pointing out to decision makers the benefits that could have occurred if evaluation had been considered initially rather than when a program is in trouble. It requires efforts by the evaluator to be involved in staff meetings and to be knowledgeable about research on topics under discussion. Evaluators should be the first to submit helpful information, using data that is available, reanalyzing and interpreting data presented, or making inferences from the literature if primary data are not available.

This may seem like a lot of work. It requires keeping up with current knowledge in the entire mental health area, which can be extremely broad. It requires interpersonal skills, since efforts by evaluators to increase involvement may be interpreted as self-serving. However, with tact and humor, marketing evaluation can be accomplished.

Step 2. Developing and Focusing Policy Questions. This is Chelimsky's first step, and it is important. When policy questions are not of major concern to policymakers, the potential use of evaluation findings is minimized and the credibility of the results jeopardized. While Chelimsky indicates that lawmakers are able and ready to establish policy areas and delineate information needs, my experience is that others are less able to do this without assistance. An evaluator who starts at an agency by asking the question "What is it that you'd like to know?" will only rarely find a decision maker who can answer. The process of identifying areas for study must be an interactive one. It can be based on discussions, brief surveys of executives, or group decision-making processes such as the Nominal Group Technique (NGT) or Delphi Technique, addressing the most significant policy areas that are likely to require information in the future.

To be able to assist decision makers in this fashion and to suggest policy questions requires the evaluator to have an in-depth content knowledge of the field. In requires being current about developments, both nationally and in other states, so that politically sensitive issues and upcoming trouble areas can be identified. It also requires sensitivity to the power structure in the agency—and whether the power structure is permanent. Pursuing a study at the urging of an executive who is not likely to remain in power may mean that interest in an evaluation study will not be permanent. As an example, one of our bureau directors urged a study of a new management technique of contracting with community mental health (CMH) boards. She departed abruptly, and interest in her study waned. On the other hand, there was a department director who left shortly after he commissioned several evaluation studies on the mental health of the aged. Unlike the first example, and perhaps because an aging constituency outside the department was well established, interest in these studies continued.

Another issue relevant to the topic of policy making is the pros and cons of in-house evaluators seeking outside funding for research projects. Priority topics and time frames for federal grants are rarely congruent with those of decision makers. Thus externally funded research projects are often outside the realm of the policy questions that local decision makers ask. In deciding to pursue a research grant application, the evaluator must weigh the positive advantages associated with obtaining outside resources and the long-range benefits of a comprehensive research investigation against the very real possibility that the research project will take away attention and resources from the needs at hand. This may also cause the evaluator to be viewed as self-serving.

Step 3. Planning and Designing the Evaluation. This activity involves taking an identified policy question and developing it into an evaluation study. It is as much an art as it is a demonstration of the evaluator's competency and technical knowledge. To be successful, evaluators must use their knowledge of the system and of the program being studied and ask the following questions:

- What is practical and feasible?
- Who are the stakeholders?
- What are the time constraints?
- Is this study really important?
- What resistances are likely to be encountered in implementing the design, and is executive-level support strong enough to overcome these resistances?
- What are the costs in time, money, and person-power to conduct the evaluation?
- What compromises are feasible?

To plan and design the most appropriate evaluation (in terms of quality, timing, efficiency, and political soundness), it is usually necessary to have numerous discussions with field and executive staff to understand the program or service to be studied and the expectations of the study. Once a preliminary plan is developed, discussions are necessary with stakeholders, as well as with those who have requested the evaluation or who may be impacted by its results. These discussions should address what the evaluation should produce, its limitations, and its conclusions. It is often useful to have a small work group established to help refine the final details of the evaluation design. This gives better input and also increases ownership of the project.

Problems associated with this step are, first, the frustration of not knowing all the feasibility and stakeholder issues and, second, how to plan an optimal design that balances the need for quality with the constraints of timeliness and efficiency. The latter problem may be particularly troublesome.

Step 4. Conducting the Evaluation. This activity includes implementing the design and analyzing the data—the part of the process for which an evaluator is best prepared. However, even here there are several important considerations that must receive attention.

First, as Chelimsky points out, interpretations of results must be decision oriented. The evaluator should not think that a purely descriptive study will be useful. An evaluation report that merely analyzes results and concludes by saying, "We do not know if this outcome is good or bad" will not be useful. Moreover, evaluations should avoid findings that contain no anchors for comparison. Consider a statement such as "Fifty percent of geriatric hospital patients have physical health problems of a chronic nature." Is such a statistic to be interpreted as high or low? Some standard must be included as part of the evaluation design and used in the analyses for comparison purposes. Standards may include a control/comparison group, normative data, census data, data from previous studies, and the quantified expectations of program initiators. Decision makers will expect the evaluator to interpret the results in prescriptive terms.

Achieving credibility for the evaluation is a second major issue the evaluator should be concerned about. Does the project staff have competency and experience in the content area as well as in the methodology of conducting evaluations? Are there personality conflicts among evaluation program staff and those being evaluated? If so, perhaps other evaluators should be chosen or credibility enhanced by adding a university collaborator or an outside consultant to the staff. An advisory committee might also add credibility to the evaluation if its members are acknowledged leaders in the content area being studied and the methods being used. Such a group can be helpful with problem solving and in acting as facilitators. In conducting evaluations of multiple sites, we often use a work group or advisory committee composed of the following: a liaison from each program site plus representatives from central office, other state government agencies, outside organizations, and advocacy groups that are interested or are key players for utilizing results.

Another major issue in conducting evaluations is how to continually involve decision makers so that their interest is not lost and so that they will be primed to use the study's results at some future time. Their participation on advisory committees can help. However, top-level executives rarely have enough time to attend such meetings. Possible alternatives might be periodic short individual meetings or one-page briefings on the project's status.

Finally, in carrying out the evaluation, the evaluator must demonstrate high technical standards of scientific merit and statistical analysis. Even though most stakeholders may not appreciate the importance of removing biases through random assignment or of whether the data fit assumptions required for discriminant function analysis, it is important not to neglect these technical points, because someone in the audience will understand them. An evaluation with a seriously flawed methodology will have limited instrumental uses and may even damage conceptual uses by casting doubt on the evaluator's credibility.

The costs for conducting evaluations involve time and skill development. Setting up advisory groups and holding individualized meetings with executive staff and other key decision makers takes a lot of time. Running effective meetings is not a skill taught in graduate school; it is one that requires personal effort to develop.

Step 5. Translating Findings. This activity focuses on knowledge and communication and has both technical and interpersonal aspects. The technical aspects are those that improve communication, such as making the findings clear, avoiding jargon, and using visual materials such as narratives and tables. Data presentations must be thorough and they often should be appendicized or made available on request. Executives and legislators rarely have time to study numerous detailed tables. Pie charts and simple graphs that are visually appealing are much more persuasive. Lately, our reports have used word tables with good success. Executive summaries are a necessity.

The interpersonal aspects of communicating are equally important. On a simple level, this involves greater use of verbal presentations rather than reliance solely on the report itself. Presentations should be short and interesting and produce meaningful interaction. Frequent personal contacts with critical players may be necessary, for example, phone calls when results are ready or occasional allusions to results in luncheon conversations or during discussions on other matters. Interpersonal contacts can have an impact on conceptual uses of evaluations by building a positive image of the evaluator, maintaining involvement, marketing the evaluation service, and shaping the decision maker's thinking on this subject.

The use of case studies and anecdotal data is helpful in making others understand and utilize evaluation results. People only understand what has meaning. Sometimes, even beautifully drawn and colored bar graphs have no meaning. However, a story may help, if it is understandable; long after the facts and figures fade from memory, people often remember an illustrative story. While decision makers are far too sophisticated today to accept case studies instead of facts and figures, the presentation of empirical results followed by an illustrative case example or anecdote can reinforce meaning. This is something of an art, for one must be sensitive to the values, biases, and perspectives of the audience in order to select an appropriately illustrative and convincing, but not misleading, case study.

The skills required to present information in anecdotal format may be nontraditional. For instance, presentations that are both appealing and persuasive might require experience in or exposure to the techniques of journalism and commercial art. Verbal skills may need reshaping, since the most effective presentations are often different from those used in academic arenas.

Step 6. Making People Pay Attention to Evaluation Results. This activity relates most to instrumental uses of evaluations. It is the final step in ensuring utilization, and one that is obviously most important. It represents the culmination of all the previous steps.

An important ingredient in ensuring an evaluation's use is knowledge about the legislative, state, or agency decision-making processes to be impacted. Of course, timing is critical. Knowledge about when budgets are submitted and decided on, when public hearings are held, and when board memberships or executive leadership changes occur is essential. Release of reports or presentation of results needs to be coordinated with the timing of these major events. If not, results may be overlooked, and attention will be given to other issues.

The evaluator's knowledge about the players, the power bases, and the dynamics of the system is also important. If an evaluator expects evaluation results to have a systemwide impact, then someone has to be willing and sufficiently interested to act on them—for instance, to implement recommended changes in policy, procedures, priorities, funding, and so on. This can happen when there is an executive who has line responsibilities and who finds the evaluation results compatible with his or her own philosophy. For instance, several years ago there was an internal debate in our department about whether geriatric mental health placements should go to specialized nursing homes or to dispersed beds in general nursing home settings. We presented an evaluation of a project that demonstrated the success of community mental health staff in providing consultation to general nursing homes on behavioral problems of residents. The results were compatible with the philosophy of the operations staff member who favored the dispersed bed notion. He quickly stepped in, disseminated and publicized the results, and used them to argue for the development of policy and funding priorities to support this program and to stop further initiatives in specialized nursing home development.

Having an agent who has operational responsibilities readily available and who is willing to use the results is an easy way to ensure utilization. However, unlike the example cited above, this does not happen often. It sometimes can be achieved by persuading operations staff that by following the recommendations of the evaluation, some other outcome may be achieved for which they are responsible—for example, the mandates of a consent decree, the concerns of a key legislator, or compliance with externally imposed standards.

The indirect use of evaluation results is more common, but still may not occur frequently. Operationally involved people are often too busy with day-to-day issues. Recommendations for change are seen as additional burdens. When this occurs, what can evaluators do? Should they drop the issue, wait for a more opportune time, or seek another course? Fortunately, there are alternatives to executive action for initiating change, namely advocacy groups and the legislative branches of state and national governments.

Advocacy groups can be powerful forces for change, especially if they are well connected to key legislative leaders. The best procedure for working with these groups is to recognize them as stakeholders and have them represented on the advisory committee or work group from the start of the evaluation. Then they will naturally receive the study's results. Giving them personal attention when explaining the results, interpreting the implications, and offering to meet with or make presentations to the group's members can produce a significant outside influence on the executive staff to carry out the recommendations of the evaluation report. Sometimes this is an even more effective way to ensure utilization than depending on the internal operations staff itself.

Obtaining legislative influence may be more difficult, since there is usually a strongly enforced separation between executive and legislative branches of governmental groups. Therefore, legislative staff would rarely be acceptable as members on advisory committees. In many agencies, there is a prohibition against any staff but the director even talking to legislators.

If one is employed by an agency (versus having a contractual relationship), the activities described above may be seen as power tactics and not approved. In many instances, penalties may be invoked. Certainly a loss of trust and confidence will result. In fact, some attempts at influencing advocacy groups may be seen as negative. However, if the evaluator feels that the possible costs can be justified, such actions are worth consideration and may help ensure that people pay attention to evaluation results.

Finally, there are occasions when there are neither operations staff interested in the results nor concerned advocacy groups or legislative interests. Perhaps these evaluation projects should never have been undertaken in the first place, or perhaps the evaluator must temporarily shelve the report, and then present it at a more opportune time. But, even if such is the case, there is another alternative. The evaluator can become the change agent. The evaluator (assuming agency agreement) can take the lead in initiating efforts to translate policy recommendations into implementable actions and can undertake training or write the standards and procedures. This utilization choice is perhaps most costly for evaluators, for once operational responsibilities have been assumed, it may be very difficult to delegate them to others. Evaluators may become staff specialists for a given content area and be relied on by other staff, so that they no longer have the time to carry on evaluative activities. Assuming the role of a change agent is risky business. However, there are some strategies and circumstances in which it may be possible to assume such a role for a limited time and still maintain or return to the evaluator function. As an example, in 1985 we carried out a research project on the homeless. Some of our major conclusions were that this population has multiple problems and that service needs must be addressed through an interdisciplinary, multiagency perspective. When it came time to implement the recommendations, there were no staff members responsible for this population nor was there a constituency of citizens or legislative interests. When our department director asked us how to proceed, we suggested an interdepartmental task force. I volunteered to spearhead and to staff this effort, since I knew that turning it over to other staff might have produced failure and since no one else had the interest or knowledge required for the job. The effort has broadened to include establishing demonstration projects for the mentally ill homeless, thus reinvolving us in evaluation. However, attention to this problem has burgeoned. Because of the major emphasis on homelessness, numerous other departmental staff have become interested and, in the near future, my responsibility can be transferred to other, more appropriate operations staff. Then my major efforts can be directed toward being an evaluator and not a staff specialist on the homeless.

Several other issues are relevant for ensuring that people pay attention to evaluation results. One issue identified by Chelimsky is that of release of early findings. She questions the appropriateness of this practice, citing the costs of presenting erroneous conclusions based on unrepresentative early information. My own position is less definitive. I agree with Chelimsky in cases where there is a chance that trends from early results may be reversed. However, we have conducted studies where the early results were so clear-cut and definitive that the advantages of optimizing timing or of meeting an executive or legislative request outweighed the possible hazards.

Another issue (not addressed by Chelimsky) should also be acknowledged. What should be done about results that are used but misquoted, extended beyond their real meaning, or overgeneralized beyond the limitations of the study's methodology? In such cases, the evaluator should clearly inform the party making the statement about the errors. The extent to which the evaluator objects is dependent on whether there is a question of gross misinterpretation of the results. If the intended outcome is generally compatible, making an issue over the matter may alienate the very stakeholders that the evaluation's recommendations are intended to influence.

An example of the above situation occurred in my division when we evaluated several demonstration projects targeted at providing support to families of developmentally disabled (DD) youngsters. Our results showed many positive outcomes but it did not show that the projects prevented a single institutional placement or brought even one child home from a facility. However, a year later proponents of a bill to give subsidies to families of the developmentally disabled who maintained these children at home repeatedly cited our evaluation report to support their contention that the subsidy would save the state money by avoiding or terminating DD institutional placements.

Conclusion

Utilization of evaluation findings presents many challenges and choices to evaluators. It also places many demands on their time and requires the development of skills and abilities far beyond those taught them as part of their graduate education. I believe that meeting this challenge is worth the time and effort expended, because failure to use evaluation results, instrumentally or conceptually, means a failure of the evaluation itself. Just as we make every effort to secure resources or to make design modifications to ensure that the evaluation is effective, so should we act to maximize its utilization. If this takes us away from the traditional skills, activities, and roles of the professional evaluator, we will be so much the better for having broadened our perspectives and our competencies.

References

Chelimsky, E. "What Have We Learned About the Politics of Program Evaluation?" *Evaluation Practice,* 1986, *8* (1), 5-21.
Chelimsky, E. "The Politics of Program Evaluation." In D. S. Cordray, H. S. Bloom, and R. J. Light (eds.), *Evaluation Practice in Review.* New Directions for Program Evaluation, no. 34. San Francisco: Jossey-Bass, 1987.
Nagel, S. S. "Factors Facilitating the Utilization of Policy Evaluation Research." Paper presented at the annual meeting of the Evaluation Research Society, Chicago, October 1983.
Rich, R. F. "Selective Utilization of Social Science Related Information by Federal Policy-Makers." *Inquiry,* 1975, *13* (3), 239-245.

*Carol T. Mowbray is director of the research and evaluation
division within the Bureau of Clinical and Medical Services,
Michigan Department of Mental Health. Her most important
contributions to the field of psychology have focused on
community psychology in the public policy area and
fall mainly in the areas of research and mental health
administration. She also has continuing interests in
women's mental health and homelessness.*

*The role of internal evaluators in large organizations continues
to expand. Several difficult and complex issues related to
evaluator functions are emerging. In this chapter these issues
are reflected on by evaluators who represent multiple
perspectives along the continuum of external to internal
evaluation.*

Business Perspectives on Internal/External Evaluation

*Oliver W. Cummings, Jeri R. Nowakowski,
Thomas A. Schwandt, R. Tony Eichelberger,
Kimball C. Kleist, Colleen L. Larson,
Tara D. Knott*

As the training function in business matures and grows more sophisticated, formal evaluation approaches will play a major role in quality
assurance for educational/training programs. Houston (1986) identified
companies such as Boeing, Disney, Motorola, and Arthur Andersen &
Co. for whom evaluation is explicitly integrated into training efforts.
Brandenburg and Smith (1986, p. 2) refer to evaluation as "a function
critical to HRD [human resource development]."

Three ways that companies can provide needed evaluation services
are by using

1. An *external* procurement strategy in which management contracts
with evaluators that are not permanent employees of the company and
are independent of the project team and program managers.

2. A *departmental* strategy in which an internal (to the company)
group that is independent of the project team and program managers is
formed as a department.

3. An *internal,* embedded strategy in which a project team member or

J. A. McLaughlin, L. J. Weber, R. W. Covert, and R. B. Ingle (eds.). *Evaluation Utilization.*
New Directions for Program Evaluation, no. 39. San Francisco: Jossey-Bass, Fall 1988.

program personnel are responsible for designing and conducting the evaluation.

It is important as businesses consider these options that administrators address issues related to the quality and effectiveness of the evaluation as well as the dollar cost of having the evaluation done.

A six-person team was assembled to consider some historically significant evaluation practice and use issues surrounding internal and external evaluators. A further aim was to explore whether these issues represent significant problems as evaluation practice has matured. In order to expand and provide context-sensitive reactions to the key issues, three professors of evaluation, R. Tony Eichelberger, Jeri R. Nowakowski, and Thomas A. Schwandt, developed a set of questions to be addressed by a group of three evaluation practitioners (one to represent each of the three previously defined strategies for providing evaluation services). The professors are all contributors to the evaluation literature and are familiar with the issues surrounding internal evaluation. They also all practice evaluation, in addition to teaching and writing. The three evaluation practitioners are all experienced, academically prepared evaluators who know first hand the practical and political complexities of doing evaluation in business settings. These practitioners are Tara Davis Knott, an external, independent evaluator; Kimball C. Kleist, manager of an internal, independent evaluation department; and Colleen L. Larson, a manager and internal evaluator, responsible for program development, implementation, and evaluation.

This team of two groups was asked to think through the difficult issues surrounding the internal evaluator's role and function. Some problems faced by the internal evaluator have been identified in evaluation literature. For example:

• Internal evaluators' objectivity may be affected by their frame of reference; they may be less able to challenge basic organizational or program assumptions, and internal evaluators' credibility might be lower than externals' (Nevo, 1983; Patton, 1986; Weiss, 1972).

• Internal evaluators may become public relations tools of the administrators; they may confuse the interests of individual managers or administrators with those of the organization (House, 1986; Patton, 1986).

• Internal evaluators may foster utilization of the evaluation process and thus reduce the usefulness of the evaluation results (House, 1986).

On the other hand, internal evaluators sometimes have the following distinct advantages in an organization:

• Internal evaluators may reduce evaluation costs (Beer and Bloomer, 1986; Patton, 1986).

• Internal evaluators allow for quick correction to evaluation designs when the evaluation activity is not productive (Cronbach and others, 1980).

• Internal evaluators may build a strong credibility over time and can more easily promote use of results and obtain stakeholder commitment to the process (Beer and Bloomer, 1986; Patton, 1986; Weiss, 1972).

• Internal evaluators help build or ensure an institutional memory for a program (Patton, 1986).

• Internal evaluators know more about the nuances and inner workings of the organization (Patton, 1986; Weiss, 1972).

These and other issues, most of which directly affect usability or propensity of clients to use evaluation results, were raised by the academic team and responded to by the practitioners from their unique perspectives. The questions posed were classified into four categories: (1) the evaluator's role, (2) evaluation methods, (3) objectivity, and (4) ensuring quality of the evaluation. Within each of the categories, the questions or issues raised are presented, and the responses from the three practitioner perspectives are given.

Evaluator's Role

The role the evaluator assumes and the relationships of the evaluator to the client influence the types of evaluations that will be done and the uses to which evaluation results can or may be put.

Cronbach has advocated an internal role for the evaluator.
Do you agree with him?

Internal evaluator: I believe there is a need and a place for both internal and external evaluators. The question is not which is better, but rather which evaluator can function most effectively and provide the most usable results given the situation. Internal evaluators have a responsibility to bring in external evaluators when they're better suited to complete the task.

Departmental evaluator: Generally, I agree with Cronbach's position. Having an internal endeavor will increase access to specialized knowledge that may be useful to product developers. When there is the risk that an internal evaluator will be perceived to be biased or to be operating in an area where they lack credibility it may be better to go to an external evaluator.

External evaluator: I disagree with Cronbach. First of all, I think his orientation is toward social programs in which the evaluator's role is to improve program effectiveness through recommendations. Accountability, according to Cronbach, is not a major concern for evaluation. In business, however, accountability is an extremely important concern. Evaluators who work in business and industry often are asked to assess program effectiveness, either to aid management in making decisions about program continuation or to show that a program works for promotional purposes. In the first instance, the internal evaluator may have conflicts of interest because of relationships with coworkers. In the second, internal evaluators' work will be suspect to potential clients if it shows that their organization's product or program is better than a competitor's. In my opinion, these roles are inappropriate for internal evaluators and can best be assumed by an external evaluator.

Does the role of the client (and thus the evaluator) change
in an internal evaluation unit so that the client is
disproportionately empowered?

Internal evaluator: Certainly, the role is different. As an internal evaluator, you are part of the team. However, this is not necessarily disproportionately empowering to the client. For example, as a manager in organizational development, my role is to assist our divisions in organizational development efforts they wish to implement. I also serve as a consultant to them in evaluating their efforts. We collaboratively engage in problem solving to define the approach that best fits the needs, interests, and concerns of the division. Their acceptance of the approach is crucial, because they will be the key players in carrying out the effort and using the evaluation results.

I am expected to hold to ethical standards and am rewarded for maintaining supportable practices within my division. When faced with a request to do something I consider unethical, I have to resolve it by going to higher management levels in the organization.

Departmental evaluator: Evaluators in our firm have responsibility to do what they, in their professional judgment, deem appropriate for a given set of circumstances. If an evaluator thinks that an indefensible approach is being recommended by a client, the evaluator has the responsibility to so advise the client and to promote the use of appropriate alternatives. On significant conflicts or concerns, the evaluator is expected to raise the issue to management levels to get the conflict resolved. Ultimately, the internal evaluator is an employee of the firm and may be expected to do work that is deemed appropriate by division management. If the department is inappropriately placed organizationally or the evaluator or evaluation management is weak, then the client may be disproportionately empowered.

External evaluator: If the "client" for internal evaluations is also the manager who formulates the budget that includes the evaluator's livelihood, he or she may be overly empowered. However, a major contractor for an external evaluator may be likewise empowered. The client's role must be overtly clarified in either situation so that the evaluator feels free to report whatever he or she finds.

Compare an external strategy and a departmental strategy in terms of costs and benefits.

Internal evaluator: The question of whether or not to hire an evaluator for internal purposes is often triggered by concerns about costs of external consultants. Certainly, if an organization doesn't do much evaluation, an external consultant may be appealing.

Internal evaluators may prove to be more cost-effective because they are readily available to respond to impromptu evaluation questions that may arise in business discussions. Having an evaluator on board also can help to spread evaluation expertise throughout the company. However, if an internal evaluator is not used, or the skills are not valued within the organization, the money would be better spent on an external consultant for a few high-interest evaluation concerns.

Departmental evaluator: Assuming a full-time need for evaluation, the cost advantage rests with the departmental approach. Efficiencies can be obtained through centralization of the function (and specialization within, for instance, data processing). Ready access to the expertise is a plus in this situation.

External evaluator: If the organization is heavily involved with evaluation, it may be more cost-effective to maintain an internal evaluation staff. Further, departmental evaluators are already a part of the corporate culture and have intimate and immediate knowledge of the real power brokers on pertinent questions. When such attributes are important, departmental evaluators might be best used.

If evaluation is only conducted on a sporadic basis, expertise could probably be procured less expensively than it could be maintained in-house. Other advantages of producing the evaluation might include specialized expertise, the introduction of a fresh "eye" for the situation, the ability to more easily access top management, and lack of loyalty to any given organizational faction.

Evaluation Methods

The positional and political influences on the evaluator differ depending on their internal or external status. These influences may impact evaluation methods, which, in turn, may significantly impact the utility of the results of the evaluation.

Are internal evaluators methodologically limited in their options?

Internal evaluator: I really don't see methodological limitation as an internal versus external issue. Certainly, methodological limitation is dependent on the skills of individuals, the size and availability of the evaluation team, and the willingness of the client to support new evaluation designs. But I would think these limitations would permeate all evaluation environments.

Departmental evaluator: No. If they are successful in communicating the benefits of a particular approach, and the client agrees that the outcomes will be worth the effort and investment, then anything goes.

External evaluator: No, in fact, internal evaluators may have more opportunity to enlighten their organizations to varied methodologies than do external evaluators. Further, internal evaluators might better maintain interest in evaluation results if they are collected and presented via different methodologies. For example, an advocate/adversary model is a good way to ensure interest in the presentation of evaluation results if the audience intimately involved with the project or program and does not require a formal report. An external evaluator may be less able to convince the client that any "nontraditional" approach is valid.

Do internal evaluation systems risk routinization? What is the value and risk of formalized and relatively rigid methodology in internal evaluation?

Internal evaluator: Certainly; routinization is always a risk of formalizing methods, tasks, or procedures. Businesses do this readily to make operations more cost and time efficient. External consultants equally do it to decrease their time investment in proposal writing and materials preparation.

Formalization is not necessarily bad; however, the term *rigid* connotes an inflexible formalization. Lack of flexibility or ability to adapt to the demands of new issues and unique problems may well result in evaluation that is not responsive to unique client needs and, consequently, not used. That, of course, would be bad. Unfortunately, people do sometimes fall into the trap of trying to fit problems to formalized methodologies rather than using appropriate methodologies to address identified problems. Evaluators must be encouraged to think. The danger of a "rigid" structure is that people will cease thinking beyond the "accepted approaches" because they soon find they are not rewarded for thinking but for following. Formalized methodologies should merely help to make the process more fluid because it documents what we know. The danger is when it is viewed as "all we know" or "all that matters."

Departmental evaluator: Yes, there is some risk associated with routinization. Any organization is interested in obtaining maximum efficiency through regularly employed procedures. If those regularly employed procedures lead to routinized responses to interviews or questionnaire items by program staff or to lowered use of the evaluation results, then there is a problem. Routinization, however, does not always need to have a negative connotation. If procedures that are routinely employed are sound, data sources change periodically, and results are used, then the only risk that is run is in the area of employee morale (assuming that purposes and context of evaluations are relatively stable). Morale should not pose significant problems either. There are few individuals that cannot be challenged in evaluation design or instrumentation and who cannot improve on what they have done in the past, even if the task is basically the same. Management has a responsibility for helping to spark creativity within constraints.

External evaluator: Although most of us have a preferred approach, the variation in contracts and sponsoring organizations probably encourages external evaluators to attempt various approaches. The internal evaluator, however, must operate within a prescribed, rather predictable context. For example, an internal evaluator might know that he or she is responsible for an annual evaluation of each ongoing management development program. That sort of repeated task could become routinized—especially if top management wants the same report in the same format each year. Further, if the evaluator is also a program staff worker, his or her evaluation time and expertise is likely to be rather limited, which could also lead to routinization.

One value to formalized or routine procedures is that a data pool of salient information could be established and used to detect trends and changes over time. Such data could improve the usefulness of evaluation results and encourage utilization. Further, once a specific methodology is entrenched, other, perhaps less experienced, evaluators could take over some of the evaluation implementation. This would free more experienced evaluators for other tasks.

A major disadvantage of a formalized methodology is that the consistent use of one or two methodologies could result in missed information about important program aspects. For example, a qualitative approach might yield useful results that the repeated use of the same quasi-experimental approach might fail to uncover.

Objectivity

The evaluator's objectivity is a critical issue in producing balanced, accurate, useful evaluation results. Objectivity in study design, data gathering, and analysis, while necessary, is not sufficient. A conviction by the evaluators to report results and promote their effective use is also needed.

How does an internal evaluator (in either a departmental or embedded strategy) establish and maintain a reputation for independence and objectivity? How do internal evaluators avoid biting the hand that feeds them?

Internal evaluator: My objectivity, as for any evaluator, rests in the evaluation process used and data gathered. I see evaluation as one part of the development process. It is one more tool to use to help us better attain our goals. I posit evaluations as a process for problem identification and resolution. We don't identify problems to place blame. We identify problems to seek solutions. My professional competence and expertise rest in producing an evaluation that is reliable, confirmable, and useful. I am biting the hand that feeds me if I don't produce and promote the use of those kinds of results.

Departmental evaluator: Objectivity is demonstrated by telling it like it is. It is ensured by establishing and following quality assurance guidelines for evaluation design and through balanced reporting of evaluation results. Independence is a relative thing. Internal evaluators and product developers all work for the same entity and are vested in the production of quality programs. Organizational sanction and management support (and perhaps protection) for the independent evaluation function is essential. The single best way for internal evaluators to avoid biting the hand that feeds them is to try to push sponsorship of the evaluation to a high enough level in the organization that the primary client is one who clearly wants a full and impartial view of the program or project. It is this client who will most likely use the evaluation results appropriately as well.

External evaluator: I think internal evaluators must establish a reputation for being "fair and tough." Otherwise, they will stand a good chance of being co-opted by political and/or peer pressures. Of course, this active attempt at objectivity or independence may result in the loss of friends and the trust of coworkers! Unless limited to formative evaluation, internal evaluators must occasionally risk biting the hand that feeds them. Therefore, internal evaluators must learn to present solid information as a basis for negative results.

Does less bad news travel upward in in-house evaluation?

Internal evaluator: Bad news might not travel upward in an in-house evaluation system if the people involved are fearful of consequences. This may be true if the evaluators feel compelled to report only good news or news that coincides with management's perceptions. This situation could be magnified if the performance of the evaluator is evaluated by the people they fear delivering bad news to. Likewise, external evaluators may not deliver bad news if they are fearful of unpopular outcomes or of not being engaged for additional services. In both situations, the result may be inaccurate or incomplete reporting of evaluation information. If the evaluation is properly placed in the organization and is well planned and executed, this problem should not arise.

Departmental evaluator: In the formative evaluations we do, the bad news is what program developers and evaluators are trying to find, so, there is no problem at all. We do emphasize balanced reporting—that is, reporting the positive and the negative. Since most of our summative (go/no-go) evaluations are on vendor programs, we do not have the internal status on them and therefore have few problems. On the occasional sensitive study we do, we try to get the project sponsored at a high enough level in the organization that the sponsor would not benefit from having bad news screened.

External evaluator: Less *formal* bad news may travel up; however, the informal news that does get to top management during an internal evaluation may be more fragmented and less reliable than that which is formally obtained and/or presented. Internal evaluators, therefore, should probably make a concerted effort to explain to management the possibility of hearing premature or otherwise tenuous bits of information before the formal report is presented. External evaluators may be more able to maintain a formal relationship with management. External evaluators should make every effort to ensure that staff persons as well as management have ownership in the evaluation; this will increase the likelihood that information (bad or good) that reaches management will not be subterfuged by staff persons or lower levels of management.

Ensuring Quality of Evaluation

Potential users of evaluation results should exercise their responsibility to ensure that they receive results of sufficient quality and usefulness. Whether in selecting an evaluator or in taking steps to ensure the quality of an evaluation, the client, as a potential user, and the evaluator, as a provider of information, share responsibility in the definition and assessment of needed skills and procedures.

What criteria should be used to choose an external, independent evaluator, and how should his or her performance be evaluated?

Internal evaluator: It is not uncommon to find people in organizations who know nothing about evaluation; therefore, they are at the mercy of any consultant who comes in claiming to be an evaluator. Further, because people know little about evaluation, there is sometimes a tendency to underestimate the need for skilled competence. Internal evaluators can be helpful in educating organizations on evaluation issues. But if an outside evaluator is to be retained, any internal evaluation expertise should be used to help assess the skills of the external evaluator.

The evaluation skills that are sought must correspond with the needs of the evaluation. For example, an evaluation that will be highly interactive will require an evaluator not only with technical skills but with strong interpersonal skills, facilitation/mediation skills, and considerable expertise in negotiation. The evaluator should be capable of exploring data for multiple meanings and should be comfortable with having people in the organization participate in the evaluation. The evaluation must be open. We would want to see the raw data. We would want to see how the evaluator categorizes qualitative information. Not all evaluators would be comfortable with, or capable of, this kind of open evaluation approach.

Departmental evaluator: Management should look at the evaluator's track record, review products, and assess the evaluator's interpersonal ability. A formal agreement, detailing activities and deliverables expected from the project, should form the basis of evaluating the evaluator's performance.

External evaluator: Track record and expertise requirements are the major criteria to use in purchasing evaluation expertise. Management should talk with others for whom the evaluator has worked and, if possible, review past work. The registry suggested by Scriven in the early 1980s is a good idea regarding an evaluator's track record. Further, an organization might need an evaluator who has specific expertise (such as tests and measurement) that would become a major criterion on which to select an evaluator. Other criteria might include the evaluator's familiarity with the field of the evaluand, professional reputation, and cost.

Performance might be judged by the degree to which the information needed was actually obtained in a valid manner and presented (or agreed to contractually) in a timely and understandable form. Other dimensions such as value for cost, technical adequacy, professionalism, and ability and availability to clearly answer questions following the conclusion of the evaluation are also important and can be used to judge the evaluator's performance. Ideally, a meta-evaluation should be conducted; however, time and budget restraints might preclude this arrangement.

How is the quality of evaluations in an embedded or departmental strategy monitored and evaluated? Who is responsible for this quality control?

Internal evaluator: At Helene Curtis we have set up our evaluation to go through both our planning and administration committees at different points in the evaluation. This is not unlike quality review checks built in proposals by external consultants. However, I believe it is rare to find that the people responsible for the quality review are knowledgeable of evaluation methodology and procedures. Typically, they are vice-presidents or managers who know their content and are interested in the project but offer little in the way of technical review.

Departmental evaluator: Quality assurance is maintained through the skills and professional development (continuing education) of the evaluator and through review of engagement memos (study design proposals) and reports by management within the evaluation group. Generally accepted standards for conduct of work, evaluation models, standards, internal methodologies, and management judgment form the basis for these reviews.

External evaluator: It is my experience that internal quality control may be somewhat slack. Criteria that are probably always applied include the degree of usefulness and timeliness for decision making. Criteria such as adherence to standards or to a recognized methodology may or may not be used to judge internal evaluations, depending, again, on the expectations and expertise of the clients and/or the personnel responsible for oversight.

Finally, if quality control does take place, it is probably the responsibility of the head of the department (departmental) or the project director (embedded). Unless the department is an evaluation department, quality control may be inadequate because the department head in, say, training or the project director may not have specific evaluation expertise by which to judge the evaluation or the evaluation may be judged by standards that are more applicable to another discipline, such as experimental research.

To what extent is the quality and value of information generated in an evaluation affected by whether the evaluation is carried out by an internal or external evaluator?

Internal evaluator: I believe that the quality and value of information generated in an evaluation is highly dependent on the skills of the evaluator. Assuming equal skills, internal evaluators may be able to dig deeper, faster because they are intimately involved with the content and the issues. There would be no learning curve for them to overcome as they begin the evaluation. However, they must also be careful not to let this knowledge unduly guide the evaluation process.

Departmental evaluator: Quality is driven by evaluator competence. Value is driven by the extent to which the client is disposed to use the results of the evaluation (the evaluator may be able to influence value somewhat through user-friendly reporting of findings). Except for the rare instance where the evaluator's perceptions are unduly affected by contact with the organization or by an overly empowered client, the fact that the evaluator is internal or external should not matter.

External evaluator: If the information that was needed to make a decision is accurate and delivered on time, the value of the information probably does not really vary depending on whether the evaluator is internal or external. The perception of the information's value may, however, increase if the evaluator is external—that is, the "outside" expert.

If an internal evaluator has good evaluation knowledge and skills, the information quality is probably high. Conversely, if the external evaluator is ill trained, the quality of the information he or she provides may be quite low. Except for the client's perceptions of the value of the information, there is probably no real difference between internal and external evaluators regarding value or quality of information.

Regardless of strategy, what skills must an evaluator possess to function effectively in a business or industry environment?

Internal evaluator: Sense of urgency—deliver when you say you will. Speak the client's language (both verbal and written). Understand the business world. Don't be tied to a methodology but be able to adapt to company needs and constraints. Know when to say you are out of your area of expertise.

Departmental evaluator: Evaluators should have good technical and interpersonal skills. The technical skills include expertise in a variety of study designs, instrument development, data gathering and analysis techniques, and excellent writing skills. Interpersonal skills include tact, communication skills, rapport building, listening skills, selling or persuasion skills, and so on. Evaluators also must be flexible. There is no room for dogmatic attitudes (except with respect to the appropriateness of dogmatic attitudes). They should have project management skills, planning and executing projects on a timely, cost-effective basis, and an understanding of and acceptance of business motives. A "consultant" mentality, knowing the client and their business problems and concerns, is also required for long-run success.

External evaluator: Aside from a good knowledge of evaluation premises and methodologies, evaluators who function in a business context must become and remain aware of management's priorities. This is now what evaluators are typically taught—that is, most evaluators are (rightfully) concerned with how well a program works for its consumers; however, they fail to recognize the importance of managers as a consumer group. For example, the bottom line may be more important to the evaluator's managerial client than the "social good" obtained by the evaluand. So evaluators in business must learn to tease out the needs and wants of managers as well as program clients and/or staff.

A conscious effort to provide information on time and with the most efficiency is also extremely important and appreciated in business and industry. Deadlines are crucial in business and industry, since in business those who don't deliver the right product at the right time have short careers. Further, business evaluators should be able to communicate clearly with all levels of management and to relate conclusions to practical recommendations. They should also make an effort to learn some of the business's jargon so that they understand what is actually being said and can respond to questions appropriately.

Summary

There are many issues that organizations and evaluators need to consider in selecting a strategy for accomplishing needed evaluation activities. Most of these issues bear more or less directly on the utility of evaluation activity and utilization of results.

We brought together six evaluators—three professors (and some-time practicing evaluators) representing the academic side of the discipline, and three practitioners, fully employed as internal or private independent evaluators. The professors posed a number of questions to which the practitioners responded. In general, there was strong agreement among the professors about what issues should be raised and among the practitioners about the meaning and conclusions to be drawn about the issues. Regardless of the practicing evaluator's position (internal, departmental, or external), most questions led to consideration of the same variables, even though the points of view occasionally were divergent.

A review of the content of the responses to the questions posed yielded the following nine recurring themes in the practitioners' answers:

- Evaluator competence and performance record
- Selective use of internal and external evaluators to capitalize on organizational awareness and meet independence needs
- Objectivity, credibility, and bias
- Accurate, balanced reporting
- Specialization of skills and efficiency
- Cost of evaluation
- Flexibility and use of multiple methods
- Organizational placement of the evaluation function
- Quality assurance and review of work.

While there is some overlap between these themes and the issues specifically addressed in the academicians' original questions, the themes and issues are not identical. Evaluation competence and performance record was the most frequently occurring theme, followed closely by selective use of internal and external evaluators and objectivity and credibility. All three of the practitioners touched on these themes repeatedly in their responses. On the other six themes there were more varied references, with some practitioners raising them more frequently than others. Yet, all three practitioners raised each remaining theme at least once in their responses to the questions. Each of these areas offers the potential for future research in the internal/external evaluation consideration.

In regard to the four categories (role, methods, objectivity, and quality assurance) into which the questions were categorized, there was agreement that the evaluator's role may be significantly influenced depending on whether the person is a consultant or an employee. It was also generally agreed that, except in unusual circumstances, most of the role issues could be appropriately controlled by the evaluator and organization management. When the evaluator's role involves the appearance of conflicting interests (for example, an internal evaluator doing summative evaluation on a peer's programs), the utilization of results is threatened. However, when an internal role is appropriate, the evaluator may be able to promote the appropriate use of evaluation results more effectively than an external evaluator.

Whether internal evaluators would be constrained in the methods they used was a significant issue for the academic questioners. The practitioners, while recognizing both positive and negative potentials for routinization of methods for either internal, departmental, or external evaluators, uniformly indicated that the internal evaluators were not constrained in methods by virtue of their positions. Thus constraints on methodology should not be a limiting factor in promoting evaluation utilization.

The area in which the greatest difference was noted between internal and external evaluators was in issues of the appearance of objectivity, sometimes related to credibility. Internal evaluators were recognized as holding a position in which credibility can be built over a long, productive relationship with the employer and utilization of evaluation can be developed and continually improved. However, it was also recognized that in some instances—for instance, when evaluation results are used to assess a product or services delivered to an outside client, and when the results are for the client's consumption—the internal evaluator's credibility (and therefore the utility of the evaluation) is reduced by virtue of the position, regardless of the quality of the evaluation.

It was uniformly agreed that all evaluators need to have a variety of skills ranging from interpersonal skills to technical skills to project management skills. While the applications of these skills may vary from position to position, they were perceived as necessary to evaluator success. Further, quality assurance (of the evaluation) was seen as an important aspect of any evaluation project. Skills and quality assurance that yield credible, timely evaluation results enhance the usability of the results.

Citing the works of a number of writers from the late 1970s and the 1980s, Worthen and Sanders (1987) indicated various factors found to influence evaluation use. Among these influences were

- Credibility of the evaluator and the evaluation
- Evaluator's reputation
- Relevance of the evaluation to client needs

- How and how well the evaluation results are interpreted and communicated
- Degree and timing of involvement of the potential users in the evaluation
- Quality of the evaluation.

We touched on all of these factors in the discussion presented in this chapter. Evaluation utilization transcends the internal versus external evaluator issue, but the appropriate selection of an internal or an external evaluator may make the difference between a useful evaluation and one that is unused in a given circumstance.

References

Beer, V., and Bloomer, A. C. "Levels of Evaluation." *Educational Evaluation and Policy Analysis*, 1986, *8*, 335-345.

Brandenburg, D., and Smith, M. E. *Evaluation of Corporate Training Programs.* Princeton, N.J.: Educational Testing Service, 1986.

Cronbach, L. J., Ambron, S. R., Dornbusch, S. M., Hess, R. D., Hornik, R. C., Phillips, D. C., Walker, D. F., and Weiner, S. S. *Toward Reform of Program Evaluation: Aims, Methods, and Institutional Arrangements.* San Francisco: Jossey-Bass, 1980.

House, E. R. "Internal Evaluation." *Evaluation Practice*, 1986, *7*, 63-64.

Houston, W. R. (ed.). *Mirrors of Excellence: Reflections for Teacher Education from Training Programs in Ten Corporations and Agencies.* Reston, Va.: Association of Teacher Educators, 1986.

Nevo, D. "The Conceptualization of Educational Evaluation: An Analytical Review of the Literature." *Review of Educational Research*, 1983, *53*, 117-128.

Patton, M. Q. *Utilization-Focused Evaluation.* (2nd ed.) Newbury Park, Calif.: Sage, 1986.

Weiss, C. H. *Evaluation Research: Methods for Assessing Program Effectiveness.* Englewood Cliffs, N.J.: Prentice-Hall, 1972.

Worthen, B. R., and Sanders, J. R. *Educational Evaluation: Alternative Approaches and Practical Guidelines.* White Plains, N.Y.: Longman, 1987.

*Oliver W. Cummings is director of research and evaluation,
Arthur Andersen and Company, Center for Professional
Education, St. Charles, Illinois.*

*Jeri R. Nowakowski is assistant professor and director of the
Office of Educational Evaluation, Research and Policy Studies,
Northern Illinois University, DeKalb.*

*Thomas A. Schwandt is assistant professor, Center for
Educational Development, University of Illinois—Chicago.*

*R. Tony Eichelberger is associate professor, Department of
Educational Research Methodology, University of Pittsburg.*

*Kimball C. Kleist is manager in research and evaluation,
Arthur Andersen and Company, Center for Professional
Education, St. Charles, Illinois.*

*Colleen L. Larson is manager in organizational development,
Helene Curtis, Inc., Chicago, Illinois.*

*Tara D. Knott is president of Evaluation Resources
Incorporated, Memphis, Tennessee.*

*In fiscal year 1983 the General Accounting Office made 1,134
recommendations to executive branch agencies as the result of
its management performance evaluations. An analysis of 176
randomly selected recommendations showed an acceptance rate
of between 51 and 77 percent by the target agencies—a rate far
higher than evaluation literature indicates evaluators generally
experience.*

Increasing Evaluation Use: Some Observations Based on the Results at the U.S. GAO

William P. Johnston, Jr.

In fiscal year 1983 the U.S. General Accounting Office (GAO) management performance evaluations resulted in 1,134 recommendations to executive branch agencies. Based on a randomly selected sample of 176 recommendations, it is estimated that between 51 and 77 percent—depending on the form of the acceptance variable used—were accepted by the target agency (Johnston, 1986). Considering that evaluation literature typically does not show such high levels of acceptance for evaluation recommendations, it is instructive to examine GAO's work and processes for approaches, which could help increase the use of the evaluative efforts of others. In examining GAO's apparent success, this chapter introduces GAO, provides a judgmental model explaining GAO's high acceptance rate, and suggests how other evaluators might benefit from GAO's experience.

The research, views, and opinions are those of the author and do not necessarily reflect the position or policies of the U.S. General Accounting Office.

J. A. McLaughlin, L. J. Weber, R. W. Covert, and R. B. Ingle (eds.). *Evaluation Utilization.*
New Directions for Program Evaluation, no. 39. San Francisco: Jossey-Bass, Fall 1988.

The General Accounting Office

The GAO was created as an agency of the Congress by the Budget and Accounting Act of 1921. Frederick Mosher, the best-known authority of GAO, characterized it as unique because of (1) its position as an arm of the Congress, (2) the fifteen-year term to which its two top officials are appointed, (3) its independence, even from the Congress, in choosing and conducting most of its work, (4) the fact that while most of its evaluative efforts are directed at the executive branch, it does not answer to any executive branch official, and (5) the almost limitless scope of its work (Mosher, 1979). Mosher further describes GAO as the auditor of executive branch programs. However, he stresses that its reports have few similarities with the traditional financially focused audit reports prepared by private-sector certified public accounting firms. He describes the GAO reports as focusing on the quality of management, serving to hold officials accountable for the performance of the activities and programs they administer (Mosher, 1979).

Performance evaluation has emerged as the major type of GAO evaluation. In this chapter, performance evaluation is the evaluation of the activities or programs of a public organization to assess one or more of the following: (1) the control of assets and the relationship of inflows and outflows of resources, (2) compliance with statutes, regulations, contracts, and other restrictions governing the agencies in their conduct of public business, and (3) the efficient and effective use of resources in carrying out program purposes and providing services to clients (Brown, Gallagher, and Williams, 1982).

Judgmental Model Explaining GAO's High Rate of Acceptance

Because the study underlying this chapter did not explore how GAO investigations, institutional arrangements, reports, and other factors differ from those of other evaluation practitioners, reasons for any differences in levels of success can only be naively assessed. This judgmental assessment, guided by the utilization literature and the research of this investigation, however, is an important and necessary product of such an effort. As Weiss (1972) said, "There is a gap between data and action that will have to be filled in with intuition, experience, gleanings from the research literature, assumption based on theory, ideology, and a certain amount of plain guessing" (p. 125). In focusing on GAO's relative success with its recommendations, it is suggested that areas of potential explanation include the types of change addressed in GAO recommendations, its position as an outside evaluator, and its activities in promoting use of its work.

Types of Change

Considering the types of change suggested in the recommendations as a possible reason for GAO's high success rate constitutes an important departure from previous utilization studies by recognizing that the proposed change might influence acceptance. Doing so requires exploring some parts of the organization literature not heretofore examined in the context of evaluation utilization—overarching typologies suggested for classifying types of change. Homer Barnett (1964) suggested the possibility of a relationship between the proposed change and its acceptance when he wrote, "The reception given to a new idea is not so fortuitous and unpredictable as it sometimes appears to be. The character of the idea is itself an important determinant. . . . There are certain situational features connected with [the new idea] which predispose those to whom it is introduced either to accept or reject it" (p. 313). Thus, analyzing the types of change GAO recommends provides a place to start the examination of evaluation use.

Fliegel and Kivlin (1966) have contended that one of the major design problems in any analysis of change comes from the need for a typology encompassing the many kinds of changes. A review of the literature reveals six typologies for classifying types of change (Downs, 1967; Eddy, 1981; Glasser and others, 1976; Knight, 1977; Morgan, 1972; Schön, 1971). Of the six typologies, Downs's (1967)—with categories of behavior, rules, structure, and purposes—was most appropriate for use in categorizing GAO recommendations. Downs's approach is preferred for two reasons. His approach was designed with public administration in mind and therefore was the most reflective of the field. Further, only Downs, among the authorities, argues that his approach provides both a methodology for classifying types of change and a foundation for determining the likelihood of acceptance for each type of change. Downs's argument implies that each type of change faces a different probability of acceptance and is especially intriguing as a way of interpreting why there are variations in acceptance rates for evaluation recommendations.

Downs classified change in terms of whether it affected behavior, rules, structure, or purposes of the organization. He defined behavior changes as those directed at bringing the actual behavior of organization members closer to the way they would behave if they totally agreed with the organization's goals. He predicted that recommendations for behavior changes would be those most readily accepted by an organization. He defined rules as the organization's formal procedures covering how employees should act in producing the organization's product or service, in coordinating complex interorganizational activities, in dealing with those outside the organization, and in approaching allocation of the organization's resources. Downs predicted that recommendation for changes in rules would have a lower likelihood of acceptance than those recommendations for changes in behavior.

Downs defined structure in terms of a hierarchy within which there is a specific distribution of information, power, income, and prestige among the organization's members. He suggested that changes that threaten structure will be greatly resisted by those officials having the most power and capability to resist. He considered recommendations for changes in organizational structure to be less likely to be accepted than those involving rules or behavior.

Changes related to the organization's purpose represent the final category in the Downs typology. He saw these changes impacting and challenging the values underlying the broad social functions for which an organization was created. Under this category he included recommendations for changes in the longer-term policy objectives that some or all of the major subordinate units pursue in carrying out their more important functions. He also included those recommendations questioning the specific values underlying the actions organizations take in attempting to achieve their broad policy goals. Downs argued that recommendations for changes in purpose had the lowest probability of acceptance.

An analysis of the 176 GAO recommendations provides support for Downs's assertion of a continuum of change. For example, using a scoring system that rated each of the 176 recommendations on a scale of likelihood of implementation based on the target agency's reaction, 81 percent of the behavior, 39 percent of the rules, and 19 percent of the structure recommendations were judged to have a high likelihood of acceptance (the one "purpose" recommendation in the sample was collapsed into the structure category). The fact that 82 percent of the 176 recommendations were categorized as either behavior or rules, the two categories of changes most likely to gain acceptance on Downs's continuum, identifies one factor accounting for why GAO has such a high acceptance rate. Thus to the extent that a greater proportion of recommendations covered in other evaluation studies might be in the structure and purposes categories, which were found to be associated with significantly lower rates of acceptance, they might be expected to encounter more resistance to adoption.

While no quantitative data were gathered to determine if GAO recommendations are proportionally lower on Downs's continuum than other evaluation work, such a claim has been made. In Levitan's and Wurzburg's (1979) important study of federal evaluation activities, they concluded, "Virtually all GAO program evaluations include recommendations to program officials. Although the recommendations are aimed at clarifying congressional mandates and improving policy implementation, the GAO too frequently restates the provisions of the law establishing the program. It is not surprising, therefore, that following a path of least resistance, agencies usually concur with GAO recommendations, *while seldom changing their policies or plans.* . . . As a rule, [GAO evaluations] make no new discoveries and *are modest in comparison to the more comprehensive evaluation conducted by the agencies* [emphasis added]" (p. 72). Thus, while certainly not conclusive, it appears consistent with both fact and opinion to suggest that some part of the difference in utilization rates between GAO and those of other evaluators can be explained by the types of recommendations GAO makes.

GAO's Role as an Outside Evaluator

The fact that GAO is not part of the agencies it evaluates may also contribute to its success in having recommendations accepted. The utilization literature takes both sides regarding the superiority of one location over the other. For example, one group of authorities contends that internal evaluators are more likely to get their recommendations accepted than their external counterparts (Dickman, 1981; van de Val and Bolas, 1977). In contrast, another researcher could not establish that a difference in acceptance existed (Weeks, 1978).

Although the evaluation literature sometimes argues for the superiority of the inside versus the outside evaluator, the organization literature makes the opposite case. Downs (1967) views changes initiated outside the organization as being more likely to succeed. Such a case may be particularly true for changes suggested by GAO. The GAO can pick its own problems to study and its own time to do the work. The importance of having the ability to pick both the problem and the time for the evaluation is stressed in the guidance GAO evaluators receive. For example, when selecting areas to evaluate, GAO staff are directed to factor in the needs and interests of congressional and other potential users. Additionally, once an evaluation is undertaken, staff are to continue to maintain contact and keep potential users informed of the evaluation's progress. The GAO guidance recognizes the importance of timeliness and stresses timing final reports and other products "to the different stages of the legislative and budgetary process" (USGAO, 1985, p. 3-6). The GAO's outsider advantage may be further strengthened by the access it has, without insider vulnerability to organizational pressure, to the Office of Management and Budget (OMB), the media, and Congress.

In the case of OMB, circular A-50 requires all executive branch agencies to have a system in place for ensuring that GAO recommendations are given a hearing. It also requires each agency to designate a top management official to be accountable for the audit (evaluation) resolution process (USGAO, 1985, pp. 9-4-9-5). OMB also receives copies of all GAO reports and executive agency replies to GAO. The net result is to make the process of deciding whether to accept or reject a recommendation a much more formal, open, and perhaps thoughtful process than that faced by other evaluators. Specific examples of the difficulty other evaluators experience in having the results of their work discussed in the "light of day" are, as would be expected, hard to locate. Levitan and Wurzburg (1979), without citing examples, have stated that "experience so far with in-house evaluation shows that results are often not disclosed to the public" (p. 124).

Richard Brown, former Kansas state auditor, is one of the few authorities providing specific examples of suppression of evaluation results. Brown, Gallagher, and Williams (1982) charged that an evaluation of the handling of highway bid-rigging cases by the Kansas attorney general resulted in extensive pressure from powerful legislative interests to alter both the audit and the final report. In another instance he stated that an evaluation showing violations of state licensing and open meeting laws was left unused by the responsible state legislative and executive branch officials. It is unlikely that other internal or external evaluators are in as favorable a position to have their recommendations heard and acted on as is GAO.

While the work on which this chapter is based showed that direct involvement by the Congress was associated with utilization, it did not address the impact on acceptance attributable to GAO's status as a congressional agency. Mosher (1984), in his most recent study of GAO, spent a considerable amount of time exploring this relationship. Mosher saw GAO's influence increasing during the 1970s as a result of certain changes taking place in the Congress, including (1) growing assertiveness in oversight; (2) devolution of power from committee chairmen to subcommittee chairmen and then to individual members, greatly increasing requests for or use of GAO reports; (3) expansion of staff resources; (4) increased emphasis on performance and effectiveness of executive branch programs; and (5) increasing independence of individual House and Senate members from party leadership and control.

He saw the net effect of these changes as strengthening and increasing GAO's influence as well as providing a greater assurance that its recommendations would be read, used, appreciated, and perhaps forced on the target agencies. Mosher (1984) concluded that "the fact that this was so probably added to the executive branch respect, concern, and even fear of GAO in its investigations" (p. 115). Levitan and Wurzburg (1979) also noted the power of GAO and concluded that "the primary vehicles of GAO influence are the recommendations made in GAO reports and the subtle threat of GAO's presence acting to help keep administrators clean" (p. 72). Based on the above, it is not unreasonable to conclude that the relationship between GAO and the Congress enhances success rate.

A final advantage that probably accrues to GAO as an outsider is its relationship with the media. Wilson (1966), in discussing innovation in organizations, said the existence of a crisis increased the likelihood of change being accepted. He argued that the crisis escalated the cost to members who oppose the change by putting them in the position of favoring a continuation of the crisis. He also believed a crisis had the effect of shifting members' attention to organizational interests rather than allowing them to continue to focus on their normal tasks. The media plays a role in these crisis situations by its propensity to focus on the most damaging aspects of a story; it is likely that "bad press" can create a crisis for the target agency. Perhaps no other evaluation organization enjoys such favorable media relations as GAO. The combination of GAO dissemination efforts and media interest made a profound impression on Mosher when he studied GAO. Commenting on relations between GAO and the media, Mosher (1984) said, "Virtually all unclassified GAO reports, which contain summary statements in the front, are released to the press. One GAO official has said that GAO is the most popular federal agency among media people in Washington, mainly because it provides more critical information about what is 'really' going on than anyone else and also because it is reliable" (p. 158).

Mosher continues, saying that investigative reporters relish GAO reports. He also noted that columnist Jack Anderson has a reporter at GAO almost all the time and pointed to the fact that when GAO was profiled by the television program "60 Minutes," GAO, in what he views as a rare exception to the rule, was portrayed in a very favorable light. Mosher concluded that "the media provide [GAO] very important channels to the Congress, the rest of the government, and the general public" (p. 158). Thus, while difficult to measure, it is not unreasonable to believe that GAO's media connections help pressure agencies to accept the results of its work, thereby contributing to its high acceptance rates.

GAO's Activities in Promoting the Use of Its Work

A final element likely to account for GAO's high acceptance rate is its follow-up activities. Studies of evaluation use indicate that evaluators expend little effort in trying to increase the use of their work. For example, one study concluded that evaluation results "may not have theoretical relevance" to the evaluator, resulting in "less concern on the part of the evaluator about the adoption of the results within the host agency" (Davis and Salasin, 1975, p. 63). Another study reported a "reluctance" by evaluators to take the initiative in helping to get their work used and attributed this to evaluators feeling "that such activity was unprofessional" (Glasser and Taylor, 1973, p. 144). Still others reported that evaluators expect "the data or a written report" in and of itself to ensure use by decision makers, although their work showed use can be increased by evaluators actively pursuing implementation (Braskamp, Brown, and Newman, 1982).

Although other evaluators may not push for acceptance of their recommendations, GAO does. GAO has an aggressive program for keeping its recommendations in front of both Congress and the appropriate agency officials. The following incident illustrating how the process has worked was related by Mosher (1984):

> On January 21, 1981, the day after the inauguration of President Ronald Reagan, Comptroller General Staats addressed a letter to Casper Weinberger, the new secretary of defense, to call his attention to possible economies in the defense budget that had been discovered in earlier GAO studies and that had not been fully acted upon. To the letter was attached a twenty-three page paper listing and summarizing some fifteen major 'cost reduction opportunities' that, according to Staats, would amount to *several billion dollars a year of savings* [emphasis added]. The message was of a kind one might have expected from the president's budget office . . . rather than from the congressional auditor [p. 182].

Subsequent to the incident described above but prior to the time period of the recommendations sampled for this report, GAO automated its utilization tracking system. The new system requires GAO staff to make frequent checks on recommendations considered still valid but which, at the time of the previous check, had not been implemented (Results . . . , 1982). It is likely the effort GAO places on following up and looking for opportunities to capitalize on the spirit of the moment results in more utilization than is achieved by the evaluators described in much of the utilization literature.

How Others Might Benefit from GAO Experience

This chapter has suggested that GAO recommendations are accepted at a high rate because they are generally on the low end of the continuum of difficulty of acceptance hypothesized by Downs; because of GAO's status as a formal, legislatively mandated, outside evaluator; and because GAO aggressively "markets" its work.

While evaluators will not intentionally lower the threshold of their recommendations to achieve higher acceptance, understanding the role the type of recommendation plays in acceptance could be used to (1) monitor the types of change recommended versus the levels desired; (2) help ensure that higher-level recommendations receive special attention by the upper levels of management; (3) help ensure that recommendations are directed to the proper level in the organization; (4) craft better recommendations, keeping them at the lowest level on Downs's continuum consistent with achieving the changes sought; and (5) interpret differences in acceptance rates between internal units in the evaluation practitioner's organization.

Its position as an outsider provides GAO with enormous flexibility in pursuing increased use of its work. As has been suggested, it is unlikely other evaluators have such substantial resources for generating pressure for acceptance of their work. However, while other evaluators may not have as formidable resources at their disposal, they could be doing more than the literature asserts is now done. It is from such a perspective that evaluators should examine GAO's use of Congress, OMB, and the media for increasing utilization. Finally, other evaluators could benefit from the ways GAO markets its work, adopting processes that focus on increasing acceptance and watching for opportunities to bring their work to the attention of decision makers. Although the evaluation literature documents the difficulty of getting recommendations accepted, when evaluators put as much creativity and initiative into gaining acceptance for their recommendations as they put into performing the evaluation, utilization is likely to increase.

References

Barnett, H. G. "The Acceptance and Rejection of Change." In G. K. Zollschan and W. Hirsch (eds.), *Explorations in Social Changes*. Boston, Mass.: Houghton Mifflin, 1964.

Braskamp, L. A., Brown, R. D., and Newman, D. L. "Studying Evaluation Utilization Through Simulations." *Evaluation Review*, 1982, *6* (1), 114–126.

Brown, R. E., Gallagher, T. P., and Williams, M. C. *Auditing Performance in Government: Concepts and Cases*. New York: Wiley, 1982.

Davis, H. R., and Salasin, S. E. "The Utilization of Evaluation." In E. Struening and M. Guttentag (eds.), *Handbook of Evaluation Research*. Vol. 1. Newbury Park, Calif.: Sage, 1975.

Dickman, F. B. "Work Activities, Settings, Methodologies, and Perceptions: Correlates of Evaluation Research Utilization." *Knowledge*, 1981, *2* (3), 375–387.

Downs, A. *Inside Bureaucracy*. Boston, Mass.: Little, Brown, 1967.

Eddy, W. B. *Public Organization Behavior and Development*. New York: Winthrop Publishing Company, 1981.

Fliegel, F. C., and Kivlin, J. E. "Attributes of Innovations or Factors in Diffusion." *American Journal of Sociology*, 1966, *72* (3), 235–248.

Glasser, E. M., Abelson, H., McKee, M., Watson, G., Garrison, K., and Lewin, M. *Putting Knowledge to Use: A Distillation of the Literature Regarding Knowledge Transfer and Change*. Los Angeles: Human Interaction Research Institute, 1976.

Glasser, E. M., and Taylor, S. H. "Factors Influencing the Success of Applied Research." *American Psychologist*, 1973, *28* (2), 140–146.

Johnston, W. P. *A Study of the Acceptance of Management Performance Evaluation Recommendations by Federal Agencies: Lessons from GAO Reports Issued in FY 1983*. Unpublished dissertation, George Mason University, 1986.

Knight, K. E. "A Descriptive Model of the Intra-Firm Innovation Process." *Journal of Business*, 1977, *40* (4), 478–496.

Levitan, S. A., and Wurzburg, G. *Evaluating Federal Social Programs: An Uncertain Art*. Kalamazoo, Mich.: W. E. Upjohn Institute for Employment Research, 1979.

Morgan, J. S. *Managing Change: The Strategies of Making Change Work for You*. New York: McGraw-Hill, 1972.

Mosher, F. C. *The GAO: The Quest for Accountability in American Government.* Boulder, Colo.: Westview Press, 1979.

Mosher, F. C. *A Tale of Two Agencies: A Comparative Analysis of the General Accounting Office and the Office of Management and Budget.* Baton Rouge: Louisiana State University Press, 1984.

"Results—Not Reports—Best Measure of GAO's Impact." *GAO Management News,* June 15, 1982, pp. 1–5.

Schön, D. A. *Beyond the Stable State.* New York: Norton, 1971.

U.S. General Accounting Office. *Project Manual: A Guide to Selecting, Designing, and Managing GAO Projects.* Washington, D.C.: U.S. General Accounting Office, 1985.

van de Val, M., and Bolas, C. "Policy Research as an Agent of Planned Social Intervention: An Evaluation of Methods, Standards, Data, and Analytic Techniques." *Sociological Practice,* 1977, *2* (2), 77–95.

Weeks, E. C. "Factors Affecting the Utilization of Evaluation Findings in Administrative Decision Making." Unpublished dissertation, University of California, Irvine, 1978.

Weiss, C. H. *Evaluation Research: Methods of Assessing Program Effectiveness.* Englewood Cliffs, N.J.: Prentice-Hall, 1972.

Wilson, J. Q. "Innovation in Organizations: Notes Toward a Theory." In J. D. Thompson (ed.), *Approaches to Organizational Design.* Pittsburg, Penn.: University of Pittsburg Press, 1966.

William P. Johnston, Jr., is group director, general management reviews, resources, community, and economic development division of the GAO and a lecturer in government and politics at George Mason University, Fairfax, Virginia. His primary interests lie in the application of quantitative methods to evaluation research endeavors.

The most useful and possibly the cheapest form of evaluation would yield results coinciding with ongoing management procedures. While this kind of evaluation may never be fully realized, it is possible to provide a continuous stream of evaluative data and analysis by introducing evaluation into project management at its inception. This chapter outlines such an approach.

Integrating Evaluation into a Program for Increased Utility and Cost-Effectiveness

Michael Quinn Patton

One of the major evaluation standards of the Joint Committee on Standards (1981) concerns cost-effectiveness: "The evaluation should produce information of sufficient value to justify the resources expended" (p. 51). In these days of increasing cost consciousness, both government and nongovernment evaluation units are being asked to be accountable. Accountability for evaluators includes being useful at reasonable cost. This chapter suggests ways of integrating evaluation into ongoing program delivery as a strategy for both increased utility and increased cost-effectiveness. Governmental evaluation units, in particular, face severe financial constraints that require creative, integrative, and cost-effective methodological strategies.

The basic premise of this chapter is that, contrary to much methodological teaching, the measurement of program implementation and outcomes need not be independent of and separate from program activities. Indeed, such independence and separation is one of the things that drives up the costs of evaluation. It can be more cost-effective, and more useful, to integrate evaluation data collection and program activities in such a way that they are mutually reinforcing and interdependent. This chapter

J. A. McLaughlin, L. J. Weber, R. W. Covert, and R. B. Ingle (eds.). *Evaluation Utilization.*
New Directions for Program Evaluation, no. 39. San Francisco: Jossey-Bass, Fall 1988.

will explore the implications of integrating evaluation into program delivery and give examples to illustrate the effective operation of the premise that such integration is cost-effective.

Traditional Measurement Principles

Since evaluation has roots in traditional social science research, academic approaches to methods and measurement continue to influence much methodological thinking. This is true even in many governmental evaluation units, which are charged, quite explicitly, with monitoring and information functions meant to be highly practical and management oriented rather than academic or research oriented. Traditional social science notions of rigor can limit the capability of both internal and external evaluators of thinking in practical, cost-effective ways about what is really useful. This section analyzes some of the practical limitations of traditional measurement principles for the conduct of cost-effective evaluations.

It is a traditional textbook measurement principle that the measurement of the effects of a treatment (a program) should be independent of and separate from the treatment itself. Where the measurement of the treatment is integrated into the treatment itself, internal validity is threatened because of treatment contamination. One classic illustration of this concern is the problem of the effects of pre- and posttesting on evaluation of a program. For example, those participants who take a pretest may perform better in the program than those who do not take the pretest, because the pretest increases awareness, stimulates learning, or enhances preparation for program activities. Thus one analyzes the difference in performance for those who took the pretest and for those who did not take the pretest to separate out test effects.

Testing effects constitute one kind of treatment contamination. More generally, evaluators are concerned that any kind of measurement may affect outcomes in such a manner that it is difficult to separate the treatment from measurement in ways that permit clear identification of treatment effects and high internal validity. Experimental designs are aimed at controlling these measurement effects. Such designs, however, can be expensive, complex, cumbersome, and require a large number of subjects.

The problem emerges most dramatically in summative evaluation, where one is attempting to establish clear causal linkages between treatments and outcomes. Where one is attempting to definitively identify causal relationships for summative purposes, concerns about testing effects and other reactive effects are important. However, the emphasis on separating measurement from the program for the internal validity of summative designs has been overgeneralized to all kinds of evaluation. For many formative purposes and some summative designs, integration of measurement and program delivery makes good sense. This possibility is especially relevant for evaluations that are highly utilization focused (Patton, 1986). The next section provides a simple example of such integration.

Adult Learning Principles and Workshop Evaluations

Let us consider the evaluation of a one-day workshop. The purpose of using a workshop evaluation as an example is to illustrate the principle of integrating evaluation into a program at the simplest possible level. We can then apply the principle to more complex program and evaluation problems.

Consider, then, a typical training workshop where the participants are to demonstrate changes in knowledge, skills, and attitudes as a result of the workshop. The evaluation design calls for a pretest and a posttest. To implement this design, the pretest is administered as the very first item in the workshop agenda. Participants are assembled and told, "Now, before we begin the workshop, we want to administer a pretest so that we can find out how much you have benefited from the workshop."

The desired design for high internal validity would include a control group that takes the pre- and posttest without experiencing the workshop, a control group that gets the posttest only, and a treatment group that gets the posttest only. All four groups, of course, should be randomly selected and assigned, and the administration of the test should be standardized and should take place at the same time.

For scientific purposes and basic research, such elegant and complex designs have considerable merit. But for formative evaluation purposes and to inform decision makers about the reasonable effects of a program, such complicated designs are overly expensive and unnecessary.

Let me now pose a contrary example of how the evaluation might be handled—a design that fully integrates the evaluation data collection into the program delivery, in other words, a design that makes the data collection part of the workshop rather than separate from and independent of the workshop.

In this scenario, the workshop begins as follows: "We are ready to begin the workshop. The first part of the workshop involves your participating in a self-assessment of your knowledge, skills, and attitudes. This will help you prepare for and get into thinking about the things we will be covering today in the workshop."

The workshop then proceeds. At the end of the day, the workshop presenter closes as follows: "Now the final workshop activity is for you to assess what you have learned today. To facilitate that process, we are going to readminister the self-assessment that began the workshop. This will serve as a review of the workshop's content and allow you to identify what you have learned. In addition, we should be contacting you in six months to repeat this assessment, both by way of reminding you of what you learned today and of finding out how well you have retained what we have covered."

In this second scenario, the word *evaluation* is never mentioned. The evaluation data collection is still a pre- and posttest, but that instrument is explicitly and directly a part of the program. The data collection builds on adult learning principles to inform the evaluation. We know that it is typically helpful to the learning process for people to be told what they will learn so that they become prepared for the learning; learning is further enhanced when it is reinforced both immediately and over the long term. In the second scenario, the self-assessment instrument serves both the function of preparing people for learning and as baseline data. The posttest serves the dual functions of learning reinforcement and evaluation posttesting. Likewise, the six-month follow-up serves the dual functions of learning reinforcement and longitudinal evaluation. Moreover, in this second scenario, there are no control groups.

Different Perspectives on Evaluation

The difference between the two workshop evaluation scenarios is not simply a matter of what participants were told. The difference I am positing is that the two scenarios represent fundamentally different ways of thinking about and conducting evaluation. In the first workshop scenario, the evaluation is separate, independent, and directed entirely at achieving evaluation purposes. In the second scenario, the evaluation is integrated, interdependent, and directed at achieving both evaluation and participant objectives. These two differences in perspective have important implications for any evaluation design, including ongoing internal monitoring systems for government programs as well as external contract evaluations. Not the least of these implications is the cost of evaluation under the two scenarios. Subsequent real program examples will illuminate these implications.

The methodological specialist will note that the second scenario is fraught with threats to validity. It is not possible to separate the data collection from the program treatment, because the data collection is explicitly and directly part of the program treatment. However the purpose of data collection in this second scenario is a simple formative assessment of the extent to which change has occurred from the pretest (initial self-assessment) to the posttest (reinforcement self-assessment) and follow-up. If the results show low scores on the pretest and higher scores on the posttest, there is good reason to believe that the score changes resulted from the activity of the day. It does not matter how much of the measured change is due to pretest sensitization versus actual learning activities, or both, as long as the instrument items are valid indicators of desired outcomes. While not establishing clear causality, at the level of face validity and evaluation reasonableness, this approach provides useful data.

Moreover, I would argue that the evaluation costs in the second scenario are not add-on costs in terms of either time or money. When the evaluation data collected is independent of the workshop at the beginning and the end, the time and expenses allocated to that activity are clearly evaluation costs. In the second scenario, however, the data collection costs are actually program delivery costs, because the learning model, or the theory of action of the program delivery, includes participant mental preparation and reinforcement. Thus, in the second scenario the data collection is so well integrated into the program that there are no separate evaluation costs except for the data analysis itself. Under the second scenario, the administration of the pretest and posttest is a part of the program such that even if the data were not analyzed for evaluation purposes, the data collection would still take place. This means that there are no additional evaluation data collection costs, making evaluation data collection highly cost-effective.

The Principle of Integrating Evaluation into Program Delivery

The workshop scenario is an extremely simple example of what is attained by integrating evaluation into the program. With this approach, evaluation is not an "add-on" that may be dispensed with as a cost-cutting measure; nor is it a luxury to be indulged in with extra dollars. Under this logic, the data collection is integral to the program and cannot be viewed as either an add-on or a luxury. This strategy also helps keep the evaluation from becoming burdensome or viewed by staff as something for which they have no responsibility and in which they have no interest.

The principle, then, is to work with program staff in articulating a theory of action or program delivery model that logically and meaningfully includes data collection points that serve first and foremost program needs but also evaluation information needs. We have used this principle in the evaluation of the Caribbean Agricultural Extension Project. The remainder of this chapter cites examples from that project.

The Caribbean Agricultural Extension Project

The Caribbean Agricultural Extension Project is funded by the U.S. Agency for International Development (U.S. AID). The project is aimed at improving national agricultural extension services in eight Caribbean countries. With staff from the University of Minnesota and the University of the West Indies, the project has involved organizational development work with key officials in eight Caribbean countries, providing in-service training for extension staff and providing equipment, including vehicles, office equipment, and agricultural equipment.

The project was designed based on eighteen months of needs assessment and planning. The assessment and planning included establishing an advisory committee in each country as well as a regional advisory committee made up of representatives from all eight participating countries and other organizations involved in agricultural development in the Caribbean.

The contract for implementing the project with all key participants was signed in January 1983. In April 1983 a meeting of the regional advisory committee was held with a team of external evaluators. The external evaluators were chosen to represent the major constituencies of the project, these being U.S. AID, the University of the West Indies, and the Midwest Universities Consortium for International Activities (MUCIA), for which the University of Minnesota was the primary representative. Each of these three prime constituencies named one of the evaluators. The fourth evaluator was chosen for his stature in the field of evaluation, because of his commitment to user-oriented evaluations, and because he was neutral from the point of view of the other three constituencies. The stakeholders agreed he should be chair of the evaluation team to work in collaboration with the three evaluators who had been named by specific constituencies.

Prior to designing the evaluation, the evaluators met with representatives of each of these three constituencies separately, including the funding source, U.S. AID. At the April meeting of the regional advisory group, the evaluators focused three days of discussion on the criteria that could be used to determine if the project had been successful. These criteria constituted a set of questions and primary outcomes, both qualitative and quantitative indicators. Based on these discussions, the evaluators reviewed design possibilities with the fifty participants in that regional advisory meeting. The details of the design were then worked out with specific representatives of the project staff and U.S. AID.

While the evaluators in this case were external contractors, the principles that guided the evaluation are equally applicable to internal governmental monitoring units, especially with regard to gathering useful information at relatively low cost with heavy time constraints.

With this overview in mind, the remainder of this analysis will focus on how the project integrated evaluation into ongoing activities.

Rapid Reconnaissance Surveys. In 1985 the Caribbean Agricultural Extension Project initiated a farming systems approach to program development and planning. The process begins with a farming systems rapid reconnaissance survey. This means using an interdisciplinary team of agricultural researchers, social scientists, extension staff, and researchers to undertake fieldwork and interviewing for a period of ten days to identify extension priorities for a specific agro-ecological zone. The team conducts interviews with farmers, traders, processors, and others involved with agriculture in the zone. Various forms of existing data are analyzed, and the team members visit farms and agricultural support institutions. The end result is specification of the parameters of existing systems and subsystems and identification of priorities for intervention.

This process serves a critical function for needs assessment, program development, and planning. It is also, quite explicitly, an intervention in and of itself in that the process garners attention from both farmers and agricultural officials, thereby beginning the extension mobilization process. In addition—and this is the point—the rapid reconnaissance survey also serves the critical evaluation function of establishing baseline data. Subsequent data on the effects of extension and agricultural development in the zone will be compared against this baseline for evaluation purposes. Yet it would be much, much too expensive to undertake this kind of intensive rapid reconnaissance survey simply for the purpose of evaluation. Such data collection is practical and cost-effective because it is fully integrated into a critical program process.

Household Farm Management Data. Once the various farming systems are identified and the needs of farmers have been specified within those systems, the extension staff begin working with individual farmers to assess their specific production goals. This process includes gathering data about the farmer's agricultural enterprises and household income flows. With this data in hand, the extension agent can work with the farmer to set realistic goals for change and to help the farmer monitor the effects of recommended interventions. The program purpose of using this approach, called a "farm management approach," is to individualize the work of extension agents with farmers so that the agent's recommendations are solidly grounded in knowledge of the farm and household situation, including labor availability, land availability, income goals, and past agricultural experiences. These data are necessary for the extension agent to do a good job of advising farm families about increasing their productivity.

These same data are the baseline for measuring the program's impact on individual farmers for evaluation purposes. The collection of such data for farm management purposes requires training of agents and a great deal of time and effort. It would be enormously expensive to collect such data independently, solely for purposes of evaluation. However, by establishing a record-keeping system for individual farmers that serves a primary extension purpose, one has also established a record-keeping system for evaluation purposes. By aggregating the data from individual households, it is possible to analyze system-level impact over time. The data aggregation and comparative analysis is above and beyond the main program purpose of collecting the data. However, without that program purpose, the data would be much too expensive to collect solely for evaluation of the system.

Staff Reporting and Planning. As noted earlier, there is an independent, external evaluation team for this project. Based on meetings with key stakeholders, including the funder (U.S. AID), the evaluators established a design aimed at measuring the processes and outcomes of the project. This design was based on the initial project proposal as funded by U.S. AID. The program staff then used the evaluation design formulated by the evaluators to establish a detailed plan of work. This detailed plan of work is the basis for monthly staff meetings and quarterly staff reports. The evaluation priorities, clearly identified and negotiated at the beginning of the project, thereby became integrated into the program as the basis for regular staff meetings and required staff reporting. As such, the evaluation priorities stay before the staff at all times.

For example, the first element in the evaluation design focused on the project goal that in each country a national agricultural extension planning committee be established and involved in providing direction to the extension service in the country. All staff meetings began by reviewing the progress of national planning committees, and all monthly and quarterly reports included information on the activities and progress of national committees. In addition, the minutes of the national planning committees were provided to the evaluators. In the actual data collection phase, the evaluators conducted interviews to gather firsthand information about the operations and activities of the national planning committees. The point here is that program implementation and evaluation were synchronized from the beginning of each. As a result, the evaluation process improved program implementation from the very beginning by focusing staff program implementation efforts.

The evaluation constituted a framework for program planning and reporting that provided focus to staff activities. This focus became more important as the project moved forward and staff encountered many opportunities to be diverted from those primary foci. However, having organized the project work plan, staff meetings, and reporting around the key evaluation issues, the evaluation contributed substantially to keeping staff efforts from being diffused into other areas or activities that would have taken away from the primary purposes of the project. This is an example of using the evaluation process for program improvements.

At the same time, the organization, format, and content of staff progress reports is easily usable by the external evaluators because the format of those reports follows the evaluation design. In short, there is a strong interface between program planning, program delivery, and evaluation such that each supports the other. Many of the costs of evaluation are thereby reduced because they are built into other critical processes.

Integrating Internal and External Evaluations

In general, this project and its evaluation illustrate one approach to combining internal and external evaluations. In much of the evaluation literature, internal and external evaluations have been treated as mutually exclusive choices. One either did internal evaluation or external evaluation. Each approach has strengths and weaknesses.

The credibility of internal evaluators is often suspect, not least of all because internal evaluators have been known to be manipulated by superiors. Yet internal evaluation is attractive because it is typically much less expensive, and internal evaluators often have a better sense of what is relevant to the organization. However, external evaluators are typically more expensive, more credible, and less knowledgeable about what is relevant.

An internal/external combination works very well when the evaluation is well integrated into the program, as is the case with the Caribbean Agricultural Extension Project. The evaluators participated in preparing an overall evaluation design that includes guidelines for internal evaluation data collection. Thus in the Caribbean Project, the evaluation design included attention to the rapid reconnaissance surveys, the farm management data collection system, and ongoing staff reporting. The evaluation team reviewed each of those data systems at the beginning of the project and discussed with staff what would be necessary to make such data credible for external evaluation use.

Subsequently, the external evaluators have conducted fieldwork based on the internal data collection system. They have verified and given credibility to the internal data collection system, noting its weaknesses where appropriate. Their evaluation report was thus based on their independent fieldwork and heavy reliance on the internal evaluation data. The final report will be an independent external document for summative purposes. The internal evaluation data, meanwhile, is serving important formative purposes.

This combination of internal and external evaluation processes has proved useful to both program staff and funders as well as other key agricultural policymakers in the region. Moreover, a major evaluation effort with a great deal of data is able to be conducted at relatively modest cost because most of the data collection is integrated into the program rather than separated from the program.

Where the evaluation data are fully integrated into the program, there can be problems with data quality. Thus, the external evaluators must negotiate what is practical and useful while striving to have the program generate the highest quality data possible. The result is not perfect. Different situations will involve varying threats to validity and reliability. Nevertheless, the final result, in my experience, is a more

94

comprehensive evaluation than would be possible if the evaluation were conducted entirely separately and independently. Moreover—and this is the bottom line—the evaluation is useful to the primary stakeholders at a reasonable cost.

References

Joint Committee on Standards for Educational Evaluation. *Standards for Evaluations of Education Programs, Projects, and Materials.* New York: McGraw-Hill, 1981.
Patton, M. Q. *Utilization-Focused Evaluation.* Newbury Park, Calif.: Sage, 1986.

Michael Quinn Patton is a social scientist at the University of Minnesota. He is president of the American Evaluation Association and the 1984 recipient of the Myrdal Award for "Outstanding Contributions to the Use and Practice of Evaluation." He is the author of five evaluation books, including Utilization-Focused Evaluation *(1986) and* Creative Evaluation *(1987), and the editor of one* New Directions *volume,* Culture and Evaluation *(1985).*

Index

A

Abelson, H., 77, 83
Alkin, M. C., 8, 17
Ambron, S. R., 60, 73
American Evaluation Association
  (AEA), 1
Anderson, Jack, 81
Arthur Andersen & Company, 59

B

Baker, E. L., 12, 13
Barnett, H. G., 77, 83
Beer, V., 60, 73
Bennett, C., 17
Bickel, W., 10, 12, 15, 18
Bickman, L., 12, 18
Bloom, H. S., 1, 5-6
Bloomer, A. C., 60, 73
Blyth, D. A., 8, 18
Boeing, 59
Brandenburg, D., 59, 73
Braskamp, L. A., 81, 83
Brennan, N. J., 8, 18
Brown, R. D., 81, 83
Brown, R. E., 76, 80, 83
Brown, Richard, 80
Bucuvalas, M. J., 8, 13, 14, 19
Budget and Accounting Act of 1921,
  75

C

Caribbean Agricultural Extension
  Project: described, 89; household
  farm management data for, 91-92;
  integrating internal and external
  evaluations of, 93-94; rapid reconnaissance surveys of, 90-91; staff
  reporting and planning for, 92
Carlson, W. A., 15, 18
Chelimsky, E., 10-11, 12, 13, 14, 18,
  48, 49, 50, 57
Ciarlo, J. A., 14, 18
Connor, R. F., 18

Cooley, W. W., 10, 12, 15, 18
Cooperative Extension Service (CES),
  9-10, 11
Cordray, D. S., 1, 5-6
Covert, R. W., 1, 6
Cronbach, L. J., 60, 73
Cummings, O. W., 3, 59, 74

D

Daillak, R. H., 8, 17
Davis, H. R., 81, 83
Delphi Technique, 50
Dickman, F. B., 79, 83
Dornbusch, S. M., 60, 73
Downs, A., 77-78, 79, 82

E

Eash, M. J., 12, 18
Eddy, W. B., 77, 83
Eichelberger, R. T., 59, 60, 74
Evaluation agenda, 2; critical concepts of, 25, 31; development of realistic, 23-24; formation of, 21,
  22-23; interpretation of, 24-25
Evaluation Network (ENET), 1
Evaluation Research Society (ERS), 1
Evaluation utilization: boundaries of,
  10; categories for lack of, 47-48, 48;
  concepts of, 2, 4-5, 10-12; as conference topic, 1-2; criteria for
  impact studies, 7; evaluator actions
  that facilitate, 12-13, 13-14, 14-15;
  factors affecting, 72-73; as function
  of design, 16-17; intended purpose
  of, 7-8; internal and external perspectives of, 3; meaning of, questioned, 9; measurement of, 16;
  organizational actions and, 8,
  15-16; parallel to adoption theory,
  8; planned for decision making,
  9-10, 17; steps toward maximiza-
  tion of, 49-57; studies, 8
Evaluations: adult learning principles
  and workshop, 87-88, 89; conduct-